Power Plates

POWER PLATES

100 nutritionally balanced, one-dish vegan meals

Gena Hamshaw
of *The Full Helping* blog

Photography by Ashley McLaughlin

TEN SPEED PRESS
California | New York

CONTENTS

INTRODUCTION

This is a book with a simple premise: to offer you one hundred practical, flavor-packed, balanced vegan meals.

The answer to what makes a meal balanced isn't always clear these days; our culture is flooded with conflicting philosophies regarding nutrition and strident opinions about what is and isn't healthy. But one way of looking at it—and the simple principle that guides my own meal planning—is that a balanced plate of food contains some protein, some fat, and some complex carbohydrates. Each recipe in this collection offers you these three nutrients, along with an abundance of fresh produce.

The careful attention I devote to dietary balance grows out of my own experience. I've struggled to find my way with healthful eating. I have a history of food extremes, including a lengthy eating disorder and subsequent flirtations with extreme diets, detoxes, cleanses, and fads. Transitioning to a plant-based diet was a major step forward for me—a decision that spurred me to seek out quality ingredients and take good care of my body through my food choices. Looking back on my early years as a vegan, though, I see how unnecessarily strict I was and how limited my diet tended to be.

When I started to think about macronutrient balance—including quality protein, fat, and carbs in every meal—things changed. I became less susceptible to cravings and midday hunger and more confident about my food choices. I felt grounded, both physically and emotionally. After a lot of stumbling and searching, I'd found a way of approaching nutrition that was focused on long-term, sustainable well-being. And the best part was that it didn't involve overthinking or cumbersome rules.

These days, in my work as a nutritionist, I have the pleasure of supporting others as they find their own way toward well-rounded eating habits. Time and again, I see how placing an emphasis on all three macronutrients within each meal can lead to increased satiety and energy.

Getting a balance of macronutrients within meals might seem like common sense, but there are reasons why it isn't always intuitive or easy. For one thing, our convenience-driven food system tends to produce a lot of snacks and quick meals that have plenty of carbohydrates and fats but not a lot of high-quality protein. Those who are concerned with protein intake often prioritize it at the expense of carbohydrates, which leaves them low on energy. In both cases, balance is lacking.

Macronutrient balance can be a special challenge for new vegans and vegetarians. Most of us were raised with the idea that a balanced dinner plate includes an animal protein, a starch, and a vegetable. Plant-based eaters sometimes eliminate the animal protein from their diets before they've figured out how to replace it with plant proteins, like beans, hemp seeds, or tempeh. This can lead to imbalanced eating habits, nagging hunger, or seemingly inexplicable cravings.

The good news is that it's easy to craft well-rounded vegan meals; it simply takes a little knowledge and practice. For people eating a plant-based diet, obtaining protein is often a matter of pairing different ingredients together, rather than plunking a piece of meat, fish, or poultry on a plate. This involves thinking synergistically about grains, legumes, nuts, seeds, and other plant foods. These recipes are designed to inspire and guide you as you get the hang of it. Over time, you'll start to customize this approach for yourself, and planning wholesome meals will become second nature.

In the following pages, you'll find balanced, nutritious vegan breakfasts, lunches, and dinners. You won't find any appetizers, snacks, or desserts here—just main dishes that are hearty enough to hold their own. Of course, we all have different appetites and needs, which vary with our lifestyles, age, health, and activity levels. Among these one hundred recipes, some are more filling and others less so. I invite you to pair these dishes with a whole grain, a salad, or another side dish if you'd like. There's no need to feel as though the recipes have to be served on their own. Just know that they can be, as they've been designed to deliver both nutrient density and satisfaction!

Because I'm talking about macronutrients, I should clarify what this book is and isn't. First, of all, it's not a diet book. Nutrition is always on my mind when I create recipes, but this book isn't an attempt to dictate what the ideal plant-based diet should be, and the recipes aren't formulated to help people lose weight. Rather, this book is an offering of vegan recipes that are intended to help you feel nourished, whether you're a lifelong vegan or a curious omnivore.

In addition, I'm not making a statement about the optimal ratio of macronutrients. If you spend much time perusing nutrition and health information, you know that there are many theories about how much protein, fat, and carbs people should eat. My personal feeling is that there's no universal ratio; human bodies and tastes differ, as do the cultures and traditions that shape our food choices. One person might feel better eating a more carb-heavy diet, while another might thrive on eating a bit more fat. On this matter, we all do well to listen to our bodies.

What I'm suggesting is simply that considering and incorporating all three macronutrients can be a useful strategy for meal planning, in both the short term and the long term. The next time you sit down to eat, ask yourself whether you have a source of protein, a good source of healthful fat, and some high quality, complex carbohydrates. If the answer is yes, then you're working with a strong foundation.

Finally, this isn't a "high-protein" book. I'm homing in on protein because I think it's important for satiety and it sometimes gets short shrift in plant-based recipes; however, it's simply one component of a balanced diet. It's also worth saying that most Americans get too much protein, which is associated with health complications. The goal isn't to obsess over protein; it's to ensure that protein makes a steady appearance in your every day meals.

About This Book

The recipes are divided into six chapters: Breakfast, Salads, Soups, Bowls, Skillets and Stovetop, and Bakes. These are the types of meals that I return to again and again at home. Many of the recipes—for example, the Spinach and Gnocchi with White Beans (page 201), the Creamy Curried Lentils and Quinoa (page 194), and the Guacamole Quinoa Salad with Black Beans (page 73)—are designed to be quick and easy, ideal for weeknight or casual midday cooking. Others, including many of the bowls and bakes, involve a little more time and planning. Before you make any of the recipes, I recommend reading it over in full so you'll have a sense of how long it will take and what's involved. There's nothing more frustrating than getting started on a recipe and realizing it will take longer than anticipated because some components require advance prep, like tofu that needs marinating, grains that should be cooked ahead of time, or vegetables that require roasting.

The cooking process for many recipes can be sped up if you prepare certain key components in advance, such as cooked whole grains or beans, homemade dressings, and ingredients like baked tofu. I often make a bunch of these staples over the weekend so that it's easy to assemble bowls, salads, or other meals on weeknights. For some pointers on weekend prep, as well as ideas for transporting these meals to work, freezing, and more, see "Using This Book" (page 12).

Adaptation is an important part of home cooking, and I encourage you to modify and experiment with these recipes over time, making them your own. That said, it's helpful to know what a recipe is intended to taste like before you start altering it. I like Ina Garten's advice to always follow a recipe closely once or twice before you make changes so that you have a benchmark to work with. After that, feel free to modify the recipes, adding and subtracting ingredients in ways that feel right to you.

At the end of the book, you'll find a sample meal plan. It isn't prescriptive or one size fits all: it's simply there to give you an idea of how these recipes might work together in the service of balanced, flavorful, seasonal eating. I encourage you to integrate the recipes into your cooking routine in whatever way works best for you. Whether you're hoping to implement Meatless Mondays with your family or you're curious about exploring full-time veganism, the recipes will provide delicious options for the journey ahead.

These recipes are created with health, pleasure, and convenience in mind. My intent is for this book to help bring some simplicity and ease to healthful eating—something that should be intuitive but can often feel overwhelming. Many of us attend to our loved ones, profession, and responsibilities capably while overlooking our own nourishment. Unfortunately, over time, fatigue and inadequate nutrition catch up with us. I believe firmly that self-care is what enables us to care for others. May this collection of recipes give you the nourishment you need to approach your work, relationships, and life powerfully.

NOTEWORTHY INGREDIENTS

Years ago, most vegan cookbooks contained a long glossary of ingredients. Grains like quinoa and ingredients like nutritional yeast hadn't yet become household staples. In the last few years, Americans' appetite for plant-based cooking has increased dramatically, and it's not at all unusual to see buckwheat, tempeh, and even nut-based cheeses on restaurant menus, in cookbooks, and at many grocery stores. Most of the ingredients in this book will be familiar to you if you've been exploring a plant-based diet for a while. But just in case, I'll highlight some ingredients that may be new to you and explain how I use them.

Barley and Farro Barley is sold either in "whole" form (with the hull removed but the bran in place) or as "pearl barley" (with some or all of the bran removed). The latter cooks more quickly, so I use it often, even though hulled barley has more fiber and nutrition. You can use either type of barley in my recipes, depending on your priorities. Hulled barley takes twice as long to cook as pearl barley: about 40 minutes, as opposed to 20. The same goes for farro, which is also sold in whole and pearl forms.

Cashews As you'll see, cashews are one of my favorite ingredients for creating creamy texture in sauces, dressings, and soups. I typically soak them for at least 2 hours before draining and blending. If you're in a rush, you can soak cashews in boiling water, which will allow you to cut the necessary soaking time down to 1 hour or even 30 minutes.

Chipotles in Adobo Sauce Chipotles in adobo are smoked, dried jalapeño chiles that have been rehydrated and canned in a sauce of tomatoes, vinegar, and spices. They're very spicy and have a deep, smoky flavor that's irresistible in soups, chilis, enchiladas, and more. If a recipe calls for a tablespoon or two of chipotles in adobo, coarsely chop the peppers so that you can measure out a level spoonful.

You're likely to have leftover chipotles in adobo after opening a can because a little goes a long way. If you won't use the remainder within a few days, transfer to a freezer-safe container and freeze for future use.

Coconut Milk Coconut milk is a terrific alternative to full-fat dairy. It's also a staple ingredient in Southeast Asian dishes, and I often use it to finish curries or in my Coconut and Scallion Rice (page 209).

Coconut foods are rich in saturated fat, so I tend to use them moderately when possible. You'll see that many of my recipes call for ½ cup to 1 cup (120 to 240 ml) coconut milk, which means that you'll have some left over after opening a can. You can freeze leftover coconut milk in ice-cube trays or freezer-safe containers, or you can use it in smoothies and desserts.

Flours My flour of choice is light spelt flour, which combines whole grain goodness with a texture that's delicate enough to work in most baked goods. I also use regular spelt flour often, as in my Spelt Biscuits (page 49), sometimes mixed with all-purpose flour to keep the texture light and balanced.

I enjoy cooking with chickpea flour, which is versatile and high in protein. I use chickpea flour for savory crepes and pancakes, like Indian *pudla* (page 189) and egg-free frittatas;

I also use it to make my French Toast (page 57), since the flavor is a little eggy. I recommend against tasting mixtures with chickpea flour before they're cooked because the uncooked flour is really bitter.

Freekeh Freekeh is wheat that's been harvested while it's still young and green, then toasted. The toasting gives it a characteristically nutty, slightly smoky flavor. Freekeh has a texture that's slightly denser than bulgur wheat, and it cooks in about the same amount of time. It's versatile and delicious, not to mention packed with protein and fiber.

Gochujang *Gochujang* is a traditional Korean condiment that's made from fermented chiles, rice, and soybeans. It's spicy, salty, and sweet, and it adds subtle umami to recipes. You can find *gochujang* at Asian grocers or online.

Ground Flaxseed You can purchase whole flaxseed and grind them in a coffee mill or pulse them in a food processor, or you can purchase pre-ground flaxseed meal in grocery stores.

There are lots of different ways to replace eggs in vegan baking, but the simple method I've been using longest is to create a "flax egg." To do this, you simply mix 1 tablespoon of ground flaxseed with 3 tablespoons of warm water and allow the mixture to thicken before adding it to batter or dough. If a recipe calls for a flax egg, be sure to mix it at the start of the process, so that it's ready to go when you need it.

Harissa Harissa is a hot chile paste or spice blend that's commonplace in North African cooking. It's very spicy and often contains coriander, cumin, and caraway. It's not difficult to find harissa in grocery stores these days, but it can also be found in Middle Eastern markets or through online grocers.

Maple Syrup and Agave Nectar I generally like to use a touch of sweetener in dressings and sauces, including marinara sauce and vinaigrette, in order to balance their tartness. If you take a more moderate stance with sweeteners, feel free to use less or omit them from the dressings altogether.

Maple syrup is my liquid sweetener of choice, but the good stuff tends to be costly. For vinaigrettes, dressings, salsas, and tomato sauce, agave nectar is a fine substitute. For breakfast recipes, like porridges, the flavor of maple syrup can't be beat.

Miso By adding umami and salty flavors to food, miso makes a wonderful ingredient for soups, dressings, and even marinades. I love roasting kabocha squash with a miso glaze, as in my macro bowls (page 157). I prefer the mild flavor of mellow white miso, but red miso and brown miso are both fine substitutes. If you have a soy allergy or prefer to avoid soy, look for chickpea- or barley-based misos online or at natural foods stores.

Nondairy Milk For most of my recipes, you can use your favorite nondairy milk, including soy, almond, hemp, or cashew. I recommend using an unsweetened variety, so that the milk can be added to savory recipes as well as sweet ones. The only exception to using your choice is full-fat coconut milk, which I call for specifically in some recipes but is too rich for others.

Nutritional Yeast An inactive form of yeast, nutritional yeast is used for seasoning rather than leavening. It has a savory, umami-rich flavor often considered to be reminiscent of cheese. It's also packed with B vitamins and protein, which makes it a nutrient-dense seasoning choice for sprinkling on pastas, salads, and more. I use it in a lot of recipes, especially those that are meant to taste "cheesy."

Nutritional yeast is available at most natural foods stores and well-stocked supermarkets, usually in the bulk-food section or sometimes in plastic bottles; you can also order it online. It comes in two forms: "large flake" or a powder. The powdered form is easier to whisk into dressings, like Maple Mustard Dressing (see page 69), whereas the flakes are better for use as a savory topping. Either variety will work in my recipes, though I recommend keeping the flakes on hand if you can find them.

Oils Olive oil gets the most use in my kitchen. It's perfect for light sautéing and in vinaigrettes. For high-heat cooking, including roasting, or if a less flavorful oil is desirable, I call for neutral vegetable oil. My go-to choices for vegetable oil are safflower, grapeseed, and refined avocado oils, as all three have a neutral flavor and are stable at high heat. In Asian-inspired dishes, I sometimes call for toasted sesame oil, which has a deep, distinctive flavor, and for Indian fare, I often call for coconut oil.

Finally, I love to drizzle unrefined nut oils, such as walnut or hazelnut oil, on salads. Just a small amount of nut oil goes a long way in terms of flavor, so it's worth investing in a bottle (they're pricey) if you're curious. Just be sure not to heat these unrefined oils, as they're damaged at high temperatures.

Pomegranate Molasses A popular ingredient in Middle Eastern cooking, pomegranate molasses has a tangy, smooth flavor. I love contrasting it with earthy, spiced lentils in my Moroccan Sweet Potatoes (page 226). It's also great in simple vinaigrettes or dressings, and you can even drizzle it over freshly roasted root vegetables for a lively contrast of tart and sweet.

Rice For the most part, I prefer brown rice to white, both because it's more nutrient dense and also because I enjoy its earthier flavor.

That said, I also appreciate the lightness and delicacy of white basmati and white jasmine rices, and their texture is better suited to certain recipes, such as Coconut and Scallion Rice (page 209), Congee (page 54), and Golden Rice Bowls with Tofu Paneer and Vegetables (page 140).

In a few recipes, I've chosen white basmati rice because its short cooking time makes it ideal for getting a meal on the table quickly. This is the case for Rice, Beans, Tofu, and Greens (page 181) and Gentle Morning Kitchari (page 24). If you're a stickler about using brown rice, feel free to substitute it, but be aware that you'll need to cook it longer, and that the texture of the final dish may be denser than intended.

Rice Vinegar A mild vinegar, rice vinegar makes lots of appearances in Asian cooking. It comes in both seasoned and unseasoned varieties; the seasoned type is very salty and a little sweet. Whenever I call for rice vinegar, I mean the unseasoned variety, which ensures that the vinegar won't add too much additional salt to the recipe.

Salt Fine sea salt is what I use in most of my cooking, so that's what I mean when I call for plain "salt." If a recipe calls for "coarse salt," you can use either kosher or coarse sea salt.

Sun-Dried Tomatoes I love using sun-dried tomatoes in my cooking. They add saltiness, umami, and tartness in one fell swoop, so they provide an easy way to boost the flavor of an otherwise simple dish, be it pasta, grain, or a salad.

Sun-dried tomatoes are sold in two forms: either packed in oil in jars or dry. The latter may be plump and moist, but if they aren't, they need to be hydrated in hot water to soften them. Just pour boiling water over them to cover and let soak for 30 minutes, then drain well before proceeding. I prefer the dry form if they're moist, but if I can't find them, I use one of the other two forms.

Tamari Instead of regular soy sauce, I use tamari in a lot of my recipes, because it's a slightly thicker and less salty alternative. If you don't have tamari, soy sauce will work fine, and in most cases, you could also substitute Bragg Liquid Aminos. If you have a soy allergy or prefer to avoid soy, you can use coconut aminos.

When I call for tamari in recipes, I mean regular tamari, not reduced sodium. It's fine to use a reduced-sodium version; just be aware that you may need to add an extra splash or two for optimum flavor.

Tofu I use extra-firm tofu in most of my recipes, but firm tofu will also work. Whenever possible, I try to press tofu before cooking. This helps draw out moisture and ensures a nice, firm texture when you sear, sauté, or bake the tofu. I've provided instructions for pressing tofu on page 15. It's not a vital step if you don't have time, but even 20 minutes of pressing can make a difference.

Vegan Buttery Spread Vegetable oils can often be substituted for butter in recipes, but sometimes a vegan butter replacement creates stronger, more authentic results (especially in baked goods, like biscuits). I recommend the Earth Balance brand, which comes in tubs or sticks and offers a soy-free option.

Vegan Meats One of my favorite all-purpose staple recipes is a savory tempeh crumble (page 185) that's a great stand-in for sausage in pasta dishes, casseroles, scrambles, and more. It's in heavy rotation in my kitchen, but I also appreciate the convenience and utility of all of the vegan meats that are available these days, including plant-based beefy crumbles, chicken strips, sausages, and more. They provide a fast, convenient way to add protein and heft to meals.

Throughout the book, I sometimes suggest adding a vegan meat of your choice. Depending on which store-bought option you choose, you may need to cook it before adding it to a recipe. If vegan meat isn't for you, you can just leave it out.

USING THIS BOOK

In this section I offer guidance on preparing many ingredients in advance and provide a few tips on freezing, packing, and transporting foods.

Batch Cooking

Many of these recipes were created with busy schedules and weeknight cooking constraints in mind. Others—especially the bowls—benefit from some advance preparation. I usually put a few hours aside over the weekend (or whenever an opportunity presents itself) to do some batch cooking. It's easy to let things simmer and bake while I take care of other household chores.

My batch cooking routine always includes making a few pots of cooked grains and beans (I'll provide details on cooking these ingredients below), as well as a dressing or two, a batch of hummus, and sometimes a tray of roasted vegetables, baked tofu, or baked sweet potatoes. It sounds like a lot of work, but if you're simmering one pot, you might as well simmer two, and it doesn't take a lot of effort to stick something in the oven while you're at it. All involve relatively little hands-on time, and once the batch cooking is done, ingredients for multiple meals are at the ready.

Cooking Grains

Most of my meals are centered around a whole grain. I have my favorites, especially quinoa, barley, and rice, but I try to vary the grains I use as much as possible, since each offers a different texture, flavor, and micronutrient profile.

For smaller grains, like quinoa and millet, I combine the dry grain and the amount of cooking liquid required, bring to a boil, then simmer until the grain is tender. With plumper and denser grains, such as wheat or spelt berries or short-grain brown rice, I boil the grain in plenty of water, as I'd cook pasta, then drain it when it's tender. I find that this eliminates a lot of guesswork and makes a huge difference in terms of texture, preventing gummy or undercooked batches. As for the cooking liquid, I stick with plain water, rather than using salted water or broth. Later, when assembling the final dish, I add other components, such as dressings, to season the grains.

Here are my methods for cooking the grains that are featured in my recipes.

Barley (Hulled) Bring a large pot of water to boil, then stir in 1 cup (200 g) of barley. When the water returns to a boil, lower the heat and simmer, uncovered, for 45 to 60 minutes, until the barley is tender yet chewy. Drain and rinse before using. 1 cup (200 g) of dry hulled barley yields about 4 scant cups (580 g) cooked.

Barley (Pearl) Bring a large pot of water to boil, then stir in 1 cup (200 g) of barley. When the water returns to a boil, lower the heat and simmer, uncovered, for 25 to 35 minutes, until the barley is tender yet chewy. Drain and rinse before using. 1 cup (200 g) of dry pearl barley yields about 3 cups (540 g) cooked.

Brown Rice (Medium- or Long-Grain) Soak 1 cup (185 g) of rice in cold water for at least 10 minutes or up to a few hours, then drain and rinse. Combine the rice and 2 cups (475 ml) of water in a saucepan and bring to boil. Lower the heat, cover, and simmer for 35 to 45 minutes, until the rice is tender and all of the water has been absorbed. Remove from the heat and let the rice steam, covered, for 5 to 10 minutes. Fluff the rice with a fork before using. 1 cup

(185 g) of dry medium- or long-grain rice yields about 3 cups (540 g) cooked.

Brown Rice (Short-Grain) Bring a large pot of water to boil. Rinse 1 cup (200 g) of rice under cold running water, then stir it into the boiling water. When the water returns to a boil, lower the heat and simmer, uncovered, for 30 to 45 minutes, until the rice is tender yet chewy. Drain the rice, then return it to the pot. Cover and let steam for 10 minutes before using. 1 cup (200 g) of dry short-grain rice yields about 3 cups (520 g) cooked.

Bulgur Wheat Bring 3 cups (710 ml) of water to a boil, then stir in 1 cup (180 g) of bulgur. Lower the heat, cover, and simmer for 7 to 10 minutes, until the bulgur is tender. Drain off any excess water, then fluff the bulgur with a fork. Cover and let sit for 10 minutes before using. 1 cup (180 g) of dry bulgur wheat yields about 3½ cups (590 g) cooked.

Farro (Hulled) Bring 3 cups (710 ml) of water to a boil. Rinse 1 cup (200 g) of farro under cold running water, then stir it into the boiling water. When the water returns to a boil, lower the heat, cover, and simmer for 30 to 40 minutes, until the farro is tender yet chewy. Drain off any excess water before using. 1 cup (200 g) of dry hulled farro yields about 2½ cups (450 g) cooked.

Farro (Pearl) Bring 3 cups (710 ml) of water to a boil. Rinse 1 cup (200 g) of farro under cold running water, then stir it into the boiling water. When the water returns to a boil, lower the heat, cover, and simmer for about 20 minutes, until the farro is tender yet chewy. Drain off any excess water before using. 1 cup (200 g) of dry pearl farro yields about 2½ cups (430 g) cooked.

Freekeh (Cracked) Bring 2½ cups (590 ml) of water to a boil, then stir in 1 cup (200 g) of freekeh. Lower the heat, cover, and simmer for 20 to 25 minutes, until all of the liquid has been absorbed. Remove from the heat and let sit, covered, for 5 to 10 minutes. Fluff with a fork before using. 1 cup (180 g) of dry cracked freekeh yields about 2½ cups (485 g) cooked.

Millet Bring 2 cups (475 ml) of water to a boil, then stir in 1 cup (220 g) of millet. Lower the heat, cover, and simmer for about 20 minutes, until all of the liquid has been absorbed. Remove the millet from heat, fluff, re-cover, and let stand for 5 minutes before using. 1 cup (220 g) of dry millet yields about 3 cups (560 g) cooked.

Oats (Rolled) Bring 1 cup (240 ml) of water to boil, then stir in ½ cup (45 g) of rolled oats. Lower the heat and simmer, uncovered, for 10 minutes, stirring occasionally, until thick and creamy. Makes 1 serving.

Oats (Steel-Cut) Bring 3 cups (710 ml) of water to a boil, then stir in 1 cup (180 g) of steel-cut oats. Lower the heat, cover, and simmer for 20 to 25 minutes, stirring every few minutes, until the oats are creamy. Makes 3 to 4 servings.

Quinoa Bring 2 cups (475 ml) of water to a boil. Rinse 1 cup (170 g) of quinoa under cold running water, then stir it into the boiling water. When the water returns to a boil, lower the heat, cover, and simmer for 12 to 15 minutes, until all of the liquid has been absorbed. Remove from the heat and let sit for 10 minutes, then fluff with a fork before using. 1 cup (170 g) of dry quinoa yields 3½ cups (485 g) cooked.

Spelt or Wheat Berries Soak 1 cup (200 g) of spelt or wheat berries for 8 to 12 hours. Bring a large pot of water to a boil. Drain and rinse the grain, then stir into the boiling water. When the water returns to a boil, lower the heat and simmer, uncovered, for 45 to 60 minutes, until the grain is tender but chewy. Drain and rinse before using. 1 cup (200 g) of dry spelt or wheat berries yields 2½ cups (440 g) cooked.

White Rice (Basmati or Jasmine) Soak 1 cup (190 g) of rice in cold water for at least 10 minutes or up to a few hours, then drain and rinse. Combine the rice and 2 cups (475 ml) of water in a saucepan and bring to a boil. Lower the heat, cover, and simmer for 12 to 15 minutes, until the rice is tender and all of the water has been absorbed. Remove from the heat and let the rice steam, covered, for 5 to 10 minutes. Fluff the rice with a fork before using. 1 cup (190 g) of dry basmati or jasmine rice yields about 4 cups (500 g) cooked.

Wild Rice Bring a large pot of water to boil, then stir in 1 cup (160 g) of wild rice. When the water returns to a boil, lower the heat and simmer, uncovered, for 45 to 60 minutes, until the rice is puffy and tender. Drain before using. 1 cup (160 g) of dry wild rice yields about 3 cups (440 g) cooked.

Keep in mind that cooking times for grains can vary depending on the age of the grain and how dry it is. Tasting is always the best way to ensure that grains are tender. If a grain is too al dente, you can add a bit of extra water and continue cooking it; conversely, if it's tender before all of the liquid has been absorbed, go ahead and remove it from the heat and drain it.

Cooking Beans

Cooking beans from scratch has its advantages. For one thing, the beans tend to hold their shape better so they don't become mushy in recipes. Another advantage is that you can add some seasonings to the beans as you cook them. Finally, it's cheaper—though canned beans are hardly a splurge! I cook beans from scratch when I can, but I use canned beans whenever it's more convenient. These recipes generally call for beans in amounts that equate easily to a can size—typically a one 15-ounce (425-g) can—so you can choose to soak and cook from scratch or use canned.

For those times when you do choose to cook beans, here are some guidelines: Start by spreading the beans (or lentils) on a rimmed baking sheet and picking through them to remove any small stones or other debris. I'm a fan of giving all dried beans an overnight soak; this will reduce the cooking time. The following day, rinse them and put them in a clean pot. Cover with enough fresh water to cover by 3 to 4 inches (7.5 to 10 cm). If you like, throw in a strip of kombu, as this may help make beans easier to digest. Bring to a boil, lower the heat, and simmer until the beans are tender. For small beans, this usually takes 45 minutes to 1¼ hours. For larger beans, it may take 1½ hours or more.

Here's a list of cooking times for commonly used beans. These times presume that the beans were soaked prior to cooking:

Adzuki Beans 45 to 60 minutes

Black Beans (Turtle Beans) 1 hour

Black-Eyed Peas 45 to 60 minutes

Cannellini Beans 1½ to 2 hours

Chickpeas (Garbanzo Beans) 1 to 3 hours (varies widely; start checking at 1 hour)

Great Northern Beans 1½ to 2 hours

Kidney Beans 1½ to 2 hours

Navy Beans 1 to 1½ hours

Pinto Beans 1½ to 2 hours

As with grains, the cooking time will vary depending on the age of the beans, and tasting is the best way to determine doneness.

When you think the beans are fully cooked, rinse a few under cold water and try them. They ought to be tender but not mushy or waterlogged. I usually start testing beans after 1 hour of cooking.

Once the beans are fully cooked and cooled, you can store them in the fridge for 3 to 5 days. Beans also store well in the freezer.

Traditional wisdom is that beans should never be salted during cooking, as it can prevent them from softening, but I often add salt before simmering without any noticeable compromises in texture. If I'm simply batch cooking beans for bowls and salads, I don't salt them before cooking, as this allows me to focus on sauces and dressings for seasoning later on.

Cooking Lentils

Cooking lentils properly seems like it should be easy, but it's taken me a long time to get it right! Part of reason is that lentils, like all legumes, can vary in age and dryness, so one batch could take 20 minutes to cook, while another could take 30 minutes. Different varieties of lentils also require different cooking times: red and yellow lentils cook most quickly (usually in 12 to 15 minutes); brown and green lentils fall in the middle (usually 18 to 20 minutes); while French, beluga, and pardina lentils can take as long as 30 minutes.

Test lentils for doneness in the same way as beans, rinsing a few under cold water and tasting them. They should hold their shape well but be tender. I like brown and green lentils slightly on the al dente side—in my opinion, that's a lot more appetizing than mushy lentils.

To cook lentils, put them in a pot and add water to cover by 3 to 4 inches (7.5 to 10 cm).

Bring to a boil, then lower the heat and simmer until tender. Drain and rinse under cool running water before using them.

Canned lentils—usually brown or black—are also available, albeit less commonplace than canned beans. They can be substituted for home-cooked lentils in a number of my recipes.

Pressing Tofu

You don't have to press tofu before cooking it, but it gives the tofu a firmer, denser texture. It also removes excess water, allowing the pressed tofu to crisp and brown more easily when cooked. Once pressed, tofu will soak up of any marinade you use, creating a more flavorful final product. Even as little as 20 minutes of pressing is usually worthwhile.

To press tofu, simply put a block of tofu on a large rimmed plate. Set another plate on top of the tofu and weight it with a couple of heavy books or large cans of tomatoes. Let sit for at least 20 minutes, or press it for up to 8 hours at room temperature. Drain away the excess water and store the tofu in an airtight container in the fridge until you're ready to use it. It will keep for 3 days.

Cubing Tempeh, Tofu, and Root Vegetables

In most of my recipes that call for tempeh or tofu, I specify cutting the protein into cubes. I think ¾ to 1 inch (2 to 2.5 cm) is a good size; most slabs of tempeh are about ¾ inch (2 cm) thick, so that size is ideal for cubes. When working with a 15-ounce (425-g) block of tofu, this means cutting it into 32 evenly sized cubes, and for an 8-ounce (225-g) slab of tempeh, it means a total of 24 cubes. You can make your cubes bigger or smaller if you prefer, and in a few recipes I do specify a smaller size.

The same goes for vegetables that are to be roasted: I usually recommend cutting sweet potatoes and other root vegetables into ¾- to 1-inch (2- to 2.5-cm) pieces for roasting, but if you prefer smaller cubes, that's fine. The main goal is to cube ingredients evenly, so all of the pieces will be fully cooked at the same time.

Freezing

The soups, stews, and many of the baked recipes in this book—including the enchiladas (page 217), stuffed shells (page 218), penne primavera bake (page 229), and lentil tamale pie (page 234)—freeze well. Having frozen dishes on hand is a great way to make life a bit easier during hectic times. So although I generally only cook for one, I always make soup and stew recipes that yield four to six servings, or even eight, rather than scaling back those recipes. I freeze half of the soup or stew, usually in individual portions, and thaw them as needed for speedy homemade lunches and dinners.

Likewise, I use my freezer to make the most of weekend batch-cooking projects. When I make a giant pot of beans or whole grains, I typically freeze smaller portions—1 to 2 cups (240 to 475 ml) once they've cooled. Then, the next time I need to quickly throw together a meal like a bowl or a salad, I have precooked ingredients to work with. The only trick is to remember to thaw them in advance!

Packing and Transporting

Nearly all of the recipes in the Skillets and Stovetop and Bakes chapters, as well as all of the soups, make for tasty leftovers. They're easy to pack and take to work, school, or wherever your schedule dictates. I use Glasslock brand containers for my leftovers, and I have an 8-ounce thermos that seals tightly for soup.

Salads and bowls can be trickier to transport and store, especially once they've been dressed or assembled. If you're hoping to enjoy leftovers, I recommend dressing individual portions of salad rather than the entire amount. Store the dressing separately from the other ingredients, and use a small 1- to 2-ounce (30- to 60-ml) container to transport the dressing. This will keep everything crisp and fresh until you're ready to eat.

MACRONUTRIENT BUILDING BLOCKS

So, what are macronutrients? Simply put, they're nutrients we need in large quantities, as opposed to micronutrients, like vitamins and minerals, which we require only in tiny amounts. Macronutrients provide us with energy in the form of calories, and they take three forms: proteins, fats, and carbohydrates.

Each macronutrient fulfills multiple functions. For example, carbohydrates are a source of energy for the brain; fats serve as an energy reserve, a source of insulation, and protection for our vital organs; and proteins are part of multiple tissue structures and, in the form of enzymes, play a role in countless biological reactions. Additionally, macronutrients help keep us energized and satisfied. Complex carbohydrates are converted into glucose for fuel, while protein and fat increase feelings of fullness, or satiety, after meals.

Getting a balance of macronutrients doesn't demand a formal recipe. In fact, it can be even easier to visualize if you think about combining everyday pantry items and kitchen staples. Here are some examples of vegan proteins, fats, and carbohydrates that are likely stocked in your kitchen already.

PROTEINS	FATS	CARBOHYDRATES
Beans (canned or dry)	Oils	Whole grains and grain products
Lentils (canned or dry)	Avocado and guacamole	Root vegetables
Dried peas	Nuts and nut butters	Winter Squashes
Tofu and Tempeh	Seeds and seed butters	Quinoa
Seitan	Coconut milk	Potatoes
Vegan meats	Dressings, sauces, and vinaigrettes	Beans (canned and dry)
Hemp seeds		Lentils (canned or dry)
Quinoa		Dried Peas

As you can see, there's some overlap (beans are a great source of both protein and carbohydrate), and this isn't a comprehensive list. Some vegetables—especially dark, leafy greens and broccoli—are a good source of protein, as are many types of grains, nuts, and seeds. I tend to think of legumes, soy foods, and vegan meats as being the most protein-dense options, which is why I feature them here.

You can mix-and-match one of each ingredient from the three groups to help ensure that your meals are well-rounded and nutritious. Below are some of my own favorite combinations for salads and bowls—almost always accompanied by fresh vegetables or fruits and other flourishes.

The list goes on and on. Over time, you'll continue to find and explore combinations that work for you! And remember that you don't only have to pick one food from each category. It's fine to add two protein or fat sources instead of one, so long as each macronutrient is well represented on your plate.

FAVORITE COMBINATIONS

Lentils + avocado + quinoa

Tempeh + dressing (like my maple mustard dressing) + sweet potato

Tofu + coconut milk + sweet potato

Hemp seeds + vinaigrette + quinoa

Seitan + sauce + brown rice

Black beans + guacamole + rice

Lentils + pumpkin seeds + butternut squash

Navy beans + olive oil and vinegar + potatoes

Chickpeas + bulgur wheat + tahini

Vegan "beef" crumbles + avocado + rice

Tempeh + toasted nuts or seeds + root vegetables

Vegan "chick'n" + vegan mayonnaise (or creamy dressing) + whole grain toast

maple syrup
the nuts
1 tsp vanilla
1 tsp cinnamon
pinch of salt
walnuts pecans?
hemp seeds

fruit
apples + pears
raspberries + peaches
strawberries

BREAKFAST

My breakfast tastes are a little nontraditional. I prefer savory breakfasts to sweet, in part because they offer me so much variety. I also appreciate how easy it is to pack protein into savory morning meals in the form of legumes, grains, and different pairings of greens.

This isn't to say that I don't enjoy traditional breakfast foods. I love a hot, creamy bowl of steel-cut oats in the morning, and in this chapter I'll share my favorite shortcut method for preparing them (page 23). I have a special fondness for vegan muesli, especially the version here (page 28), inspired by the creamy, tart bowls of grain, fruit, nuts, and yogurt that I used to eat at my great-aunt's home in Switzerland. And whole grain vegan waffles (page 45) are a cherished weekend ritual in my home—unless I'm cooking up stacks of hearty pancakes (page 37).

If you like muffins, porridge, pancakes, and other classic breakfast fare, you'll find plenty of options in this chapter. But you'll also find ideas for breakfast offerings that may seem unconventional, like slow-simmered vegan congee (page 54), sweet and savory baked sweet potatoes (page 58), and a vegan spin on traditional *migas* (page 38). You'll find a recipe for *kitchari* (page 24), an Indian porridge made with rice, dal, and mild spices. I've also included my favorite vegan breakfast hash (page 31), which is made with earthy, nutritious tempeh and sweet roasted root vegetables. The nice thing about these savory breakfast recipes is that they're also suitable for lunch or dinner, making them (and their leftovers) good multitaskers.

What I hope to convey with this array of recipes is that breakfast can be as diverse and playful a meal as any other; it doesn't have to feel like an afterthought or something you make on autopilot. I know that weekday mornings can be hectic, and I've provided tips on how to prepare some of the recipes in advance so you can fit them into busy and leisurely mornings alike.

SHORTCUT STEEL-CUT OATS

I love the texture of steel-cut oats, but I don't love their cooking time. Bringing them to a boil before bedtime, covering the pot, and letting them sit overnight is an easy shortcut. When I finish cooking the oats the next morning, I like to stir in some nondairy milk, along with a bit of maple syrup for sweetness and a splash of vanilla. As they're heating up, I prepare any toppings I'll need, like toasted nuts or diced fruit. At the end of the recipe, you'll find four of my favorite combinations, one for each season.

MAKES 4 SERVINGS

1¼ cups (225 g) steel-cut oats

4 cups (950 ml) water

Generous pinch of salt

½ cup (120 ml) unsweetened nondairy milk, plus more if desired

2 tablespoons maple syrup

1 teaspoon vanilla extract

OPTIONAL ACCOMPANIMENTS
See note below for seasonal suggestions

The previous evening, combine the oats, water, and salt in a medium pot. Bring to a boil over high heat, stirring occasionally. Remove the pot from the heat, cover, and let sit overnight.

In the morning, add the nondairy milk, maple syrup, and vanilla. Stir well, then place over medium-low heat. Bring to a simmer and cook, stirring occasionally, for 5 to 10 minutes, until the oats thicken. If they're too thick, add more nondairy milk until you reach a consistency you like.

Divide the oats into four bowls, add any desired toppings, and serve right away.

TOPPING SUGGESTIONS

Winter Currants, cacao nibs, and toasted, chopped walnuts or hazelnuts

Spring Chopped dried apricots, toasted pistachios, and a pinch of ground cardamom

Summer Sliced banana, sliced strawberries, and toasted coconut flakes

Fall Sliced apple or pear, almond butter, and a pinch of ground cinnamon

GENTLE MORNING KITCHARI

If I could eat one thing for breakfast every day, it might be *kitchari*, a gently spiced rice and lentil dish that holds a cherished place in Indian cooking. Also known as *khichdi*, the dish varies from region to region, but it's nearly always a combination of basmati rice and dal (dried split peas or lentils, which can be found at Indian grocers or well-stocked health foods stores). White basmati or long-grain rice will yield the best results, but if you don't have either on hand, quinoa is a good substitute.

MAKES 4 TO 6 SERVINGS

1 tablespoon coconut oil

2 teaspoons mustard seeds

1 teaspoon cumin seeds

1 white or yellow onion, diced

3 carrots, peeled and diced

1 tablespoon finely grated or minced fresh ginger, or 1 teaspoon ground ginger

¾ cup (140 g) white basmati or jasmine rice, rinsed

1 cup (200 g) dried moong dal, toor dal, urad dal, or red lentils

1 teaspoon ground turmeric

¼ teaspoon ground cloves

1 teaspoon salt

¼ teaspoon freshly ground black pepper

4 cups (950 ml) low-sodium vegetable broth

2 cups (475 ml) water

OPTIONAL TOPPINGS
Lemon wedges, chopped fresh cilantro, melted coconut oil for drizzling

Heat the oil in a large pot over medium heat. When the oil is shimmering, add the mustard and cumin seeds and cook, stirring constantly, until the seeds begin to pop, about 2 minutes. Add the onion, carrots, and ginger and sauté for about 5 minutes, until the onion is tender and translucent.

Stir in the rice, dal, turmeric, cloves, salt, pepper, broth, and water and bring to a boil over high heat. Lower the heat, cover, and simmer for 20 minutes. Remove the lid, stir well, and then simmer, uncovered, for 5 to 10 minutes, until the texture resembles porridge (for a soupier texture, decrease the cooking time, and for a thicker texture, cook it a bit longer). Taste and adjust the seasonings if desired. Serve with your toppings of choice.

EVERY DAY BREAKFAST TOSTADAS

The "every day" in the title of this recipe isn't just figurative: I eat tostadas most mornings for breakfast! They're easy to assemble, and they're a great vehicle for leftover vegetables and proteins. I use canned refried beans more often than not, but the homemade version in this recipe is simple enough to prepare if you have the time. There are countless ways to top the tostadas. I've offered a few of my favorites, but feel free to improvise.

MAKES 2 SERVINGS

REFRIED BEANS

1 tablespoon olive oil

½ small white or yellow onion, chopped

1 small clove garlic, minced or finely grated

1½ cups (270 g) cooked black or pinto beans with their cooking liquid, or 1 (15-oz, or 425-g) can

½ teaspoon chili powder

¼ teaspoon smoked paprika

¼ teaspoon salt

Freshly squeezed lime juice

Red pepper flakes or cayenne pepper

TORTILLAS AND TOPPINGS

4 (6-in, or 15-cm) corn or whole wheat tortillas

1 Hass avocado, sliced

Salsa

Shredded romaine lettuce or mixed greens

OPTIONAL TOPPINGS

Sliced smoked or baked tofu, seitan strips, tempeh sausage, tofu scramble, roasted vegetables, cabbage slaw, sliced or chopped tomato, chopped cucumber, hot sauce, chopped scallions

To prepare the beans, heat the oil in a medium skillet over medium heat. Add the onion and sauté for about 5 minutes, until tender and translucent. Add the garlic and cook, stirring constantly, for 1 minute. Add the beans and their liquid, the chili powder, and the paprika. Using a potato masher or the back of a spoon, smash and stir the beans. Lower the heat and simmer, stirring frequently, for 10 to 15 minutes, until considerably thickened. Stir in the salt and lime juice and season with red pepper flakes. Taste and adjust the seasonings if needed, then remove from the heat.

To assemble and serve the tostadas, toast the tortillas over a stove burner set to very low heat until crispy and lightly browned, 1 to 2 minutes per side, using tongs to flip them (or you can wrap them in foil and heat them in the oven at 350°F/175°C for 15 minutes). Spread each tortilla with about one-quarter of the refried beans, one-quarter of the avocado slices, salsa to taste, and a handful of romaine. Add any additional desired toppings and serve.

APPLE GINGER MUESLI

Traditional muesli isn't cooked, but thanks to an overnight soak in nondairy yogurt, the oats become amazingly soft and creamy, with a nice tart flavor. This is an ideal recipe for busy days: prepare it the night before, then grab it on your way out the door the next morning for breakfast on the go.

MAKES 2 SERVINGS

1 cup (90 g) rolled oats

1½ teaspoons finely grated or minced fresh ginger, or ½ teaspoon ground ginger

¼ teaspoon ground cinnamon

2 tablespoons shelled hemp seeds

2 tablespoons sliced or slivered almonds

¼ cup (40 g) finely chopped pitted dates or whole raisins or currants

1 small apple, grated

12 ounces (340 g) plain or vanilla nondairy yogurt

Unsweetened nondairy milk if desired

Maple syrup (optional)

In a medium glass bowl or container with a lid, combine the oats, ginger, cinnamon, hemp seeds, almonds, dates, and apple. Stir in the yogurt. Cover and refrigerate overnight.

The next morning, the muesli will be very thick and creamy. If it's thicker than you'd like, stir in nondairy milk as needed to achieve the desired consistency. Serve drizzled with maple syrup.

HASH
WITH ROOT VEGETABLES AND TEMPEH

Without the traditional meat, many vegan hash recipes leave me feeling less than satisfied. In this recipe, I pair tempeh with roasted root vegetables for a filling brunch dish that can easily cross over to dinner. A lot of hash recipes call for cooking the vegetables directly in the skillet, but I think roasting them creates better flavor.

MAKES 4 SERVINGS

2 large or 3 small russet or Yukon gold potatoes, scrubbed and cut into 1-inch (2.5-cm) pieces

4 large carrots, peeled and cut into 1-inch (2.5-cm) pieces

1 large turnip, scrubbed and cut into 1-inch (2.5-cm) pieces

1 tablespoon neutral vegetable oil

Coarse salt and freshly ground black pepper

¾ cup (175 ml) low-sodium vegetable broth, plus more if needed

1 tablespoon tamari

8 ounces (225 g) tempeh, cut into ¾-inch (2-cm) cubes

1 tablespoon olive oil

1 white or yellow onion, diced

8 ounces (225 g) brussels sprouts, shredded

1 tablespoon chopped fresh rosemary leaves, or 1 teaspoon dried rosemary

1 teaspoon smoked paprika

1 to 2 teaspoons apple cider vinegar

OPTIONAL ACCOMPANIMENTS
Baby arugula or other baby greens or steamed greens; toast or cooked quinoa or bulgur wheat

Preheat the oven to 425°F (220°C) and line a rimmed baking sheet with parchment paper. In a large bowl, combine the potatoes, carrots, and turnip. Drizzle with the vegetable oil and toss until evenly coated. Spread the vegetables on the lined baking sheet and sprinkle with salt and pepper. Bake for 35 to 40 minutes, until crispy and browning at the edges, stirring once halfway through baking.

Combine the broth and tamari in large skillet and bring to a simmer over medium-low heat. Add the tempeh and simmer for about 10 minutes, until the tempeh has absorbed all of the broth. Transfer the tempeh to a plate.

Heat the olive oil in the same skillet over medium heat. Add the onion and cook, stirring occasionally, for about 5 minutes, until translucent. Add the brussels sprouts and cook, stirring frequently, for 4 to 5 minutes, until the brussels sprouts are tender. Add the tempeh, rosemary, paprika, and vinegar to taste.

Add the roasted vegetables and stir gently to combine. If the hash seems too dry, stir in ¼ to ½ cup (60 to 120 ml) more broth. Taste and adjust the seasonings if desired. Serve right away, along with any desired accompaniments.

CAULIFLOWER SCRAMBLE

Tofu scramble is the quintessential vegan breakfast scramble, but you can also create scrambles with vegetables or beans. I like using cauliflower because it becomes crisp-tender during cooking and it soaks up spices and seasonings well. I especially like to pair it with chickpeas, which add protein and texture to this colorful morning meal.

MAKES 4 SERVINGS

1 tablespoon olive oil

1 small white or yellow onion, diced

1 red bell pepper, diced

3 cloves garlic, minced

1 small head cauliflower, chopped into small florets and pieces

⅓ cup (80 ml) water or low-sodium vegetable broth

1½ cups (250 g) cooked chickpeas, or 1 (15-oz, or 425-g) can, drained and rinsed

2 tablespoons tamari

1½ teaspoons ground turmeric

½ teaspoon mustard powder

½ teaspoon smoked paprika

1 teaspoon dried thyme

3 tablespoons nutritional yeast

½ bunch kale, stemmed and chopped into bite-size pieces

OPTIONAL ACCOMPANIMENTS
Cooked brown rice, whole grain toast, or baked sweet potatoes; Tempeh Bacon (see page 97); hot sauce; lemon wedges

Heat the oil in a large, wide skillet over medium heat. Add the onion and bell pepper and cook, stirring occasionally, for 7 to 8 minutes, until the onion is tender and golden. Add the garlic and cook, stirring constantly, for 2 minutes.

Add the cauliflower and stir to combine, then add the water. Cook, stirring occasionally, for 8 to 10 minutes, until the cauliflower is crisp-tender.

Stir in the chickpeas, tamari, turmeric, mustard powder, paprika, thyme, and nutritional yeast and cook, stirring occasionally, for about 5 minutes, until the chickpeas are warm and the cauliflower is perfectly tender and beginning to brown. Add the kale and cook, stirring constantly, until the kale has wilted. Taste and adjust the seasonings if desired. Serve right away, along with any desired accompaniments.

CREAMY BREAKFAST POLENTA
WITH STEWED FRUIT AND HEMP SEEDS

I rely on oats so much that other porridge options rarely cross my mind. I'm so glad I was introduced to breakfast polenta by cookbook author and breakfast guru Megan Gordon, whose enthusiastic words inspired me to create my own version. I like to serve it with a simple mixture of stewed fruit and hemp seeds for protein. If you don't have time to prepare the stewed fruit, you can substitute your favorite fruit preserves. You can also prepare the stewed fruit in advance and store it for up to 1 week in an airtight container in the fridge.

MAKES 4 SERVINGS

½ cup (75 g) chopped dried apricots

½ cup (75 g) chopped pitted prunes

½ cup (75 g) chopped pitted Medjool dates

1 cinnamon stick

⅛ teaspoon ground allspice

1 teaspoon finely grated or minced fresh ginger, or ½ teaspoon ground ginger

2 tablespoons sugar

1 tablespoon finely grated orange zest

¼ cup (60 ml) freshly squeezed orange juice

2½ cups (595 ml) water

2 cups (475 ml) unsweetened nondairy milk, plus more for serving (optional)

1¼ cups (175 g) polenta or medium-grind cornmeal

⅛ teaspoon salt

1 tablespoon vegan buttery spread (optional)

¼ cup (40 g) shelled hemp seeds

In a small saucepan, combine the apricots, prunes, dates, cinnamon, allspice, ginger, sugar, orange zest and juice, and 1 cup (240 ml) of the water. Stir everything together, then bring to a boil over medium heat. Immediately lower the heat, cover, and simmer, stirring occasionally, for 15 to 20 minutes, until the liquid has thickened and the fruit is soft.

Meanwhile, in a medium pot, combine the nondairy milk and the remaining 1½ cups (355 ml) water and bring to a boil over medium-high heat. Lower the heat, whisk in the polenta and salt, and simmer, stirring almost constantly, for 10 to 15 minutes, until the polenta is thick and pulling away from the sides of the pan. Stir in the buttery spread.

Serve right away, topped with the fruit compote and hemp seeds and a splash of nondairy milk.

HEARTY PANCAKES
WITH BUCKWHEAT AND BLUEBERRIES

Buckwheat flour adds protein, fiber, and a pleasantly nutty flavor to traditional morning pancakes. This recipe can be made with a combination of buckwheat flour and either wheat or oat flour. The oat flour version is gluten-free, and it's a refreshing counterpart to gluten-free pancake recipes that demand a complicated mixture of flours and starches. I like to add the blueberries to the pancakes as they cook, which keeps them from sinking to the bottom of the batter or discoloring it too much. If you'd like to keep your pancakes warm while you finish making the batch, you can preheat the oven to its lowest setting and hold the finished pancakes in the oven until all of them have been cooked.

MAKES ABOUT 8 (4½-IN, OR 11.5-CM) PANCAKES

3 tablespoons warm water

1 tablespoon ground flaxseed

2 teaspoons apple cider vinegar

1½ cups (355 ml) unsweetened nondairy milk

1 cup (120 g) spelt flour, all-purpose flour, whole wheat flour, or oat flour

½ cup (60 g) buckwheat flour

2 tablespoons sugar

2 teaspoons baking powder

¼ teaspoon salt

1 tablespoon neutral vegetable oil, plus more for the griddle

⅔ cup (100 g) fresh or frozen blueberries

OPTIONAL TOPPINGS
Seasonal berries, maple syrup, fruit compote, vegan buttery spread, chopped nuts

In a small bowl or measuring cup, whisk together the water and ground flaxseed and set aside to thicken for a few minutes. Separately, stir the vinegar into the nondairy milk.

In a large bowl, whisk together the flours, sugar, baking soda, and salt.

Add the flaxseed mixture to the milk mixture, then stir in the oil. Add to the flour mixture and stir with a spatula or whisk just until the batter is smooth; a few small lumps are okay, but it should be well combined.

Heat a griddle over medium-low heat. Lightly coat it with oil, then, using a ⅓-cup (80-ml) measure, portion the pancake batter onto the griddle, leaving a bit of space between the pancakes. Top each with 4 or 5 blueberries. Cook for about 2 minutes, until bubbles start to form on the upper surface and the edges of the pancakes can be lifted easily with a spatula. Flip and cook for 1 to 2 minutes more, until cooked through. Repeat with the remaining batter. Top as desired and serve right away.

TOFU MIGAS

I always have a lot of tortillas on hand, and sometimes they start to dry out before I have a chance to use them. This isn't a problem; it's an opportunity to make a big skillet of these vegan *migas*! The dish is similar to a typical tofu scramble, but the tortilla strips and salsa create a thick, soupy texture as the dish cooks. To round out the meal, serve the *migas* over tortillas, brown rice, or steamed greens.

MAKES 4 SERVINGS

5 (6-in, or 15-cm) corn or wheat tortillas, plus more for serving

1 tablespoon olive oil

1 large or 2 Roma tomatoes, chopped

1 small white or red onion, diced

1 red or green bell pepper, diced

1 poblano chile, finely diced

½ teaspoon smoked paprika

½ teaspoon ground cumin

½ teaspoon chili powder

¾ cup (180 g) salsa verde or other salsa

1 (15-oz, or 425-g) block extra-firm tofu, preferably pressed (see page 15)

2 tablespoons nutritional yeast

½ cup (15 g) chopped fresh cilantro (optional)

Salt and freshly ground black pepper

OPTIONAL ACCOMPANIMENTS

Lime wedges, hot sauce, chopped scallions, toasted tortillas, cooked brown rice, steamed greens

Toast the tortillas over a gas burner set to very low heat until just crispy and lightly browned, 1 to 2 minutes per side, using tongs to flip them (you can also wrap them in foil and heat them in the oven at 350°F/175°C for 15 minutes). Once the tortillas are cool enough to handle, cut them into 1-inch (2.5-cm) strips (about six per tortilla).

In a large skillet, heat the oil over medium-high heat. Add the tomato, onion, bell pepper, and poblano and cook for 6 to 8 minutes, stirring occasionally, until the onion is very tender and the tomatoes have released their juices.

Stir in the paprika, cumin, chili powder, and salsa, then add the tortilla strips and stir to combine. Cook, stirring gently from time to time, for 4 to 5 minutes, until the tortillas have absorbed most of the salsa and are starting to fall apart.

Crumble the tofu into a medium bowl, making sure not to crumble it too finely (some bite-size pieces should still be visible). Add the nutritional yeast and toss to evenly coat. Transfer the tofu to the skillet and cook, stirring occasionally, for about 2 minutes, until it's warmed through. Stir in the cilantro, then season with salt and pepper to taste. Serve right away, along with any desired accompaniments.

SAVORY OATS, TWO WAYS

Oatmeal has been a favorite breakfast for as long as I can remember, but in the last two years savory oats have become a full-blown obsession. I start with a basic mixture of oats, nutritional yeast, and finely chopped greens, then top them with those tiny leftover bits that aren't substantial enough for other uses—that last scoop of lentils, a few stray cubes of tempeh, and so on—along with a drizzle of dressing, a dollop of hummus, or a handful of chopped fresh herbs.

MAKES 2 SERVINGS

1 cup (90 g) rolled oats

1 cup (240 ml) unsweetened nondairy milk

1 cup (240 ml) water

¼ teaspoon salt

Generous pinch of freshly ground black pepper

2 cups (60 g) firmly packed baby spinach, or 1 cup (155 g) frozen chopped spinach, thawed

2 heaping tablespoons nutritional yeast

Combine the oats, water, nondairy milk, salt, and pepper in a small saucepan and bring to a boil over medium heat. Lower the heat to maintain a simmer.

Add the spinach (if using baby spinach, layer it on top of the oats, then cover and cook for about 1 minute, until the spinach wilts). Stir in the spinach and any desired seasonings (see the suggestions below) and cook, stirring frequently, for 5 to 7 minutes, until the oats are thick and creamy. Stir in the nutritional yeast, then taste and adjust the seasonings if desired.

Serve right away, topped with any of the ingredients suggested below or others you like.

SAVORY TURMERIC CHICKPEA OATS

Add ½ to ¾ teaspoon ground turmeric to the oats as they simmer. Top each bowl with about ⅓ cup (55 g) cooked chickpeas, along with a dollop of tahini, chopped fresh cilantro or scallions, chopped cashews, or any combination of those ingredients.

SAVORY MEDITERRANEAN OATS

Once the spinach has been stirred in, add ¼ teaspoon garlic powder and ½ cup finely chopped sun-dried tomatoes (25 g if dry-packed, or 55 g if oil-packed). Top each bowl with about ⅓ cup (60 g) cooked white beans or lentils, chopped fresh parsley, Smoked Paprika Hummus (page 149), Cheesy Hemp Seed Topping (page 89), crumbled crackers, Savory Tempeh Sausage Crumbles (page 185), or any combination of those ingredients.

AVOCADO AND TOFU TOASTS

Avocado toast is a mainstay in many kitchens these days, and every person has his or her own favorite recipe. I like to top mine with thinly sliced tomato and smoked tofu, which makes the toast reminiscent of an open-faced BLT sandwich.

MAKES 2 SERVINGS

4 slices bread

1 large or 2 small Hass avocados, halved, pitted, and peeled

Coarse or flaked salt and freshly ground black pepper or red pepper flakes

1 small ripe tomato, thinly sliced

4 ounces (115 g) smoked or baked tofu, cut into thin slices

Toast the bread. Mash the avocado flesh with a fork, then spread it on the toast. Sprinkle with salt and pepper. Top with a single layer of tomato slices, then a layer of tofu slices. Serve right away.

WHOLE GRAIN WAFFLES

I used to assume that making waffles from scratch was a huge undertaking, but investing in an inexpensive waffle iron and finding a recipe I loved turned my thinking around. Nowadays, these whole grain waffles are my favorite weekend breakfast. I mix the batter the night before, then cover it and refrigerate it overnight. In the morning, I add a splash of nondairy milk to loosen it up. Once the waffle iron is preheated, it's easy to have homemade waffles on the table within minutes. If you'd like to serve the waffles all at once, preheat the oven to its lowest setting and hold the finished waffles in the oven until all of them have been cooked.

MAKES 5 OR 6 (7-IN, OR 18-CM) ROUND WAFFLES

3 tablespoons warm water

1 tablespoon ground flaxseed

2 teaspoons apple cider vinegar

1½ cups (355 ml) unsweetened nondairy milk

1¾ cups (210 g) spelt flour, whole wheat pastry flour, or white whole wheat flour

½ cup (50 g) oat bran

3 tablespoons sugar

2 teaspoons baking powder

¼ teaspoon salt

3 tablespoons grapeseed or safflower oil

Vegetable oil spray, for the waffle iron

OPTIONAL TOPPINGS
Toasted pumpkin seeds, shelled hemp seeds, fresh fruit, fruit compote, vegan buttery spread, maple syrup, apple or pumpkin butter

In a small bowl or measuring cup, whisk together the water and ground flaxseed and set aside to thicken for a few minutes. Separately, stir the vinegar into the nondairy milk.

Put the flour, oat bran, sugar, baking powder, and salt in a large bowl and stir with a whisk to combine.

Add the oil and flaxseed mixture to the milk mixture. Pour into the flour mixture and stir to combine; I recommend using a whisk to prevent lumps. Let the batter rest for a few minutes as you preheat your waffle iron to medium-high heat.

Spray the waffle iron generously with vegetable oil spray. Add ½ cup (120 ml) batter, close the lid, and cook for 2 to 3 minutes, until the waffle is crispy and golden at the edges (the amount of batter and the timing can vary depending on your waffle iron). Remove the waffle, then repeat with the remaining batter, always spraying the waffle iron before adding more batter. Serve warm, with any optional toppings you like.

SKILLET-BAKED OATMEAL
WITH SUMMER STONE FRUIT

Digging into this sweet, fragrant baked oatmeal is like eating a fruit crumble for breakfast. If that's not enough to sell you on the idea, it's also a great make-ahead breakfast option and a flexible vehicle for your favorite seasonal fruit. I've made it with nectarines, plums, apples, pears, and even berries. The only trick is to adjust the baking time depending on how juicy the fruit is: longer baking times for juicy fruit, shorter baking times for less juicy fruit.

MAKES 4 TO 6 SERVINGS

3 tablespoons warm water

1 tablespoon ground flaxseed

2½ cups (225 g) rolled oats

1 teaspoon baking powder

1 teaspoon ground cinnamon

¼ teaspoon salt

2⅓ cups (630 ml) unsweetened nondairy milk

¼ cup (60 ml) maple syrup

1 tablespoon coconut oil or neutral vegetable oil

5 peaches or nectarines, peeled and cut into 1-inch (2.5-cm) pieces

3 tablespoons sugar

1 teaspoon vanilla extract

¼ cup (25 g) chopped pecans or walnuts (optional)

Preheat the oven to 350°F (175°C). In a small bowl or measuring cup, whisk together the water and ground flaxseed and set aside to thicken for a few minutes.

In a large bowl, stir together the oats, baking powder, cinnamon, and salt. In small bowl, whisk together the nondairy milk, maple syrup, and flaxseed mixture. Add to the oat mixture and stir until well combined.

Heat the oil in a 10- or 12-inch (25- or 30-cm) cast-iron skillet over medium heat. Add the peaches and let them sizzle and cook for 1 minute. Sprinkle with 2 tablespoons of the sugar and the vanilla. Cook, stirring occasionally, for about 4 minutes, until the fruit is soft and just beginning to brown. Pour the oat mixture over the fruit, then stir gently until the fruit is evenly distributed.

Bake for 20 minutes, then sprinkle the remaining 1 tablespoon sugar and the nuts over the top. Bake for about 10 minutes longer, until the fruit is bubbling in places and the surface is firm to the touch. Let cool for 5 to 10 minutes before serving.

SPELT BISCUITS
WITH WHITE BEAN GRAVY

BISCUITS

2 teaspoons apple cider vinegar or white vinegar

¾ cup (175 ml) unsweetened nondairy milk

1 cup (120 g) spelt flour

1 cup (120 g) all-purpose flour

1 tablespoon baking powder

¼ teaspoon baking soda

½ teaspoon salt

6 tablespoons (85 g) vegan buttery sticks, diced

WHITE BEAN GRAVY

1 tablespoon olive oil

1 small white or yellow onion, diced

4 cloves garlic, finely minced

1½ cups (355 ml) low-sodium vegetable broth

3 tablespoons all-purpose flour or whole wheat pastry flour

2 tablespoons nutritional yeast

½ teaspoon salt

½ teaspoon smoked paprika

1½ cups (240 g) cooked navy, Great Northern, or cannellini beans, or 1 (15-oz, or 425-g) can, drained and rinsed

1½ tablespoons fresh thyme leaves, or 2 teaspoons dried thyme

1 tablespoon chopped fresh rosemary leaves, or 1 teaspoon dried rosemary

1 teaspoon ground or rubbed sage

Freshly ground black pepper

OPTIONAL ACCOMPANIMENTS

Steamed leafy greens, Tempeh Bacon (see page 97)

Making homemade biscuits may sound challenging, but this recipe is simple and reliable. I use a combination of spelt and all-purpose flours to pack in some whole grain goodness without sacrificing that all-important light, crumbly biscuit texture. The White Bean Gravy is flavored with fresh herbs and, for umami, some nutritional yeast.

———————————————

To make the biscuits, preheat the oven to 425°F (220°C) and line a rimmed baking sheet with parchment paper. Add the vinegar to the nondairy milk and stir to combine. Put the flours, baking powder, baking soda, and salt in a large bowl and stir with a whisk to combine. Add the buttery spread and use a pastry cutter to cut it into the flour mixture until the mixture resembles a coarse meal. Add the milk mixture and stir with spatula or spoon until evenly combined.

Turn the dough onto a floured work surface and pat it out until about ½ inch (1.3 cm) thick. Use a biscuit cutter (or an empty bean can!) to cut out 6 to 8 biscuits. Transfer the biscuits to the lined baking sheet. Gather the scraps, gently knead them together, and then cut out another biscuit or two. Bake for 15 minutes, until the biscuits are fluffy and gently browning at the edges. Transfer to a wire rack to cool.

Meanwhile, to make the gravy, heat the oil in a medium pot over medium heat. Add the onion and cook, stirring occasionally, for about 5 minutes, until tender and translucent. Add the garlic and cook for 2 minutes, stirring constantly.

Transfer the onion and garlic to a blender and add the broth, flour, nutritional yeast, salt, paprika, and 1 cup (180 g) of the beans. Process until smooth, then return to the saucepan. Stir in the thyme, rosemary, and sage and cook over medium-low heat, stirring frequently, for about 5 minutes, until thick and bubbly. Add the remaining beans and use a potato masher to gently mash them into the gravy. Season with pepper, then taste and adjust the seasonings if desired.

Top each biscuit with a generous ladle of gravy. Serve right away, along with any desired accompaniments.

WHOLEMEAL MUFFINS

I love muffins, but they generally leave me hungry before too long. These wholemeal muffins are as close as I've come to finding a truly satisfying option. I often bake them, then freeze half for breakfasts in a hurry. They're great with a schmear of almond butter. When you mix the batter, it will seem impossibly, inadvisably packed with carrots, apple, raisins, and walnuts. Don't panic: the proportions are perfect once the muffins bake.

MAKES 12 MUFFINS

3 tablespoons warm water

1 tablespoon ground flaxseed

1½ cups (180 g) spelt flour or whole wheat flour

1 cup oat bran (95 g) or wheat bran (60 g)

½ cup (45 g) rolled oats or spelt flakes

2 teaspoons baking powder

½ teaspoon baking soda

½ teaspoon salt

⅓ to ½ cup (75 to 110 g) brown sugar, depending on desired sweetness

⅓ cup (80 ml) maple syrup

⅓ cup (80 ml) neutral vegetable oil

1 cup (245 g) applesauce

1¾ cups (190 g) grated carrots (about 3 carrots)

1 apple, grated

¾ cup (110 g) raisins

½ cup (50 g) chopped walnuts

OPTIONAL ACCOMPANIMENTS
Apple butter, jam, nut butter, fresh fruit

Preheat the oven to 350°F (175°C). Oil a 12-cup muffin tin or line it with paper liners. In a small bowl or measuring cup, whisk together the water and ground flaxseed and set aside to thicken for a few minutes.

Put the flour, bran, rolled oats, baking powder, baking soda, and salt in a large bowl and stir with a whisk to combine. In a small bowl, combine the sugar, maple syrup, oil, applesauce, and flaxseed mixture and stir well. Add to the flour mixture and stir just until combined. Fold in the carrots, apple, raisins, and walnuts.

Divide the batter evenly among the muffin cups. Bake for 25 to 28 minutes, until the tops of the muffins are firm and golden. Transfer the pan to a wire rack to cool for about 15 minutes, then remove the muffins and let cool to room temperature. Serve with any desired accompaniments.

CHAI-SPICED MILLET PORRIDGE
WITH CARROTS AND APPLES

Millet makes a good porridge base because it's creamy without being mushy. The carrots, apples, and dried fruit sweeten this porridge without any need for added sugar—though a drizzle of maple syrup to finish certainly won't hurt!

MAKES 4 SERVINGS

1½ cups (165 g) grated carrots (about 3 carrots)

1 small apple, grated

1 cup (220 g) millet, rinsed

3 cups (710 ml) water

½ teaspoon salt

1 cinnamon stick, or ½ teaspoon ground cinnamon

½ teaspoon ground ginger

¼ teaspoon ground nutmeg

¼ teaspoon ground cardamom

¼ cup (35 g) raisins or chopped pitted dates

3 tablespoons shelled hemp seeds

1 cup (240 ml) unsweetened nondairy milk, plus more as needed

Maple syrup (optional), for serving

Put the carrots and apple in a medium pot, then place the millet on top. Pour the water over the millet, then add the salt, cinnamon, ginger, nutmeg, and cardamom. Bring to a boil over medium heat. Lower the heat, cover, and simmer for about 20 minutes, until the millet is plump and tender and the water has been absorbed.

Remove the cinnamon stick. Add the raisins, hemp seeds, and nondairy milk and stir well. Simmer uncovered for about 5 minutes, until the millet is thick and creamy, adding more nondairy milk as needed to achieve a porridge consistency. Serve right away, along with the maple syrup.

CONGEE

This is my simple spin on congee, a traditional Asian rice porridge. It requires about an hour of simmering, but the time is inactive and the leftovers are great for any meal—breakfast, lunch, or dinner. I like congee in the morning, so I use only a moderate amount of garlic and ginger; feel free to double the amounts for more of a flavor punch. I often use tofu in place of the traditional addition of pork or chicken, but beans, edamame, or seitan strips would all be good protein options.

MAKES 4 SERVINGS

1 cup (185 g) white jasmine rice

2 cloves garlic, finely minced or grated

1 tablespoon finely minced or grated fresh ginger

¾ teaspoon salt

8 (1.9 L) cups low-sodium vegetable broth, plus more if desired

2 teaspoons toasted sesame oil or vegetable oil

3 scallions, white and green parts separated and chopped or thinly sliced

5 ounces (140 g) shiitake mushrooms, stemmed and sliced

2 teaspoons tamari

Pinch of red pepper flakes

8 ounces (225 g) smoked or baked tofu, thinly sliced into strips

Combine the rice, garlic, ginger, salt, and broth in a large pot. Bring to a boil over high heat, stirring occasionally. Lower the heat and simmer, uncovered, for 1 hour, stirring every 10 minutes or so to prevent the rice from sticking. The consistency of congee can range from a thick porridge to a loose, silky mixture that's reminiscent of soup; if it's thicker than you'd like, add more broth or water as needed to achieve the desired consistency. Taste and add more salt if you like.

After the rice has cooked for about 50 minutes, heat the sesame oil in a medium skillet over medium-low heat. Add the white parts of the scallions and the mushrooms. Cook, stirring frequently, for 5 to 7 minutes, until the mushrooms are tender. Stir in the tamari and red pepper flakes.

Divide the congee among four bowls and serve topped with the mushroom mixture, the tofu, and the remaining scallions.

FRENCH TOAST

I've tried many vegan French toast recipes over the years, each employing a different mixture of ingredients to mimic what's traditionally accomplished with eggs and milk. This recipe, which uses a simple mixture of nondairy milk and chickpea flour, hit the jackpot. No one will know the French toast is vegan unless you tell them!

MAKES 4 SERVINGS

8 thick slices day-old sourdough or country bread, ideally ½ to 1 inch (1.3 to 2.5 cm) thick

1½ cups (355 ml) unsweetened nondairy milk

3 tablespoons chickpea flour

1 tablespoon cornstarch, tapioca flour, or arrowroot powder

2 teaspoons nutritional yeast

1 teaspoon ground cinnamon

⅛ teaspoon salt

1 tablespoon maple syrup

1 teaspoon vanilla extract

4 teaspoons vegan buttery spread or neutral vegetable oil, for frying

OPTIONAL TOPPINGS

Fresh fruit, shelled hemp seeds, maple syrup

Place the bread in a shallow baking pan in a single layer. In a blender, combine the nondairy milk, chickpea flour, cornstarch, nutritional yeast, cinnamon, salt, maple syrup, and vanilla and process until smooth. Pour the mixture over the bread and let it soak up the liquid for at least 15 minutes, or cover and refrigerate for up to 12 hours.

Heat 1 teaspoon of the vegan buttery spread on a nonstick griddle over medium heat. When the griddle is hot, add however many slices of bread will fit without touching. Cook for 2 to 3 minutes on each side, until crispy and golden on both sides. Repeat as needed until all the slices have been cooked. Serve right away, with your favorite toppings.

BREAKFAST SWEET POTATOES,
TWO WAYS

Baked sweet potatoes make for a hearty and satisfying breakfast, and they're an easy option if you bake the potatoes in advance; just reheat them in a microwave or a 350°F (175°C) oven before serving. They lend themselves to both savory and sweet options. I've provided two of my favorite serving suggestions, but there are so many other ways to approach this easy breakfast. I've topped breakfast sweet potatoes with everything from leftover chili or White Bean Gravy (see page 49) to various combinations of dried fruits and nuts.

MAKES 2 SERVINGS

2 medium sweet potatoes, scrubbed and pricked several times with a fork

4 teaspoons melted coconut oil or vegan buttery spread

Salt

Preheat the oven to 400°F (200°C) and line a baking sheet with parchment paper. Put the sweet potatoes on the lined baking sheet and bake for 45 to 60 minutes, until fork-tender all the way through.

Let cool briefly, then split the potatoes lengthwise. Drizzle 1 teaspoon of the oil over the flesh of each half, sprinkle with a tiny pinch of salt, and then use a fork to mash the flesh, still in the skin. Top with the ingredients suggested below, or as desired.

BREAKFAST SWEET POTATOES WITH YOGURT AND GRANOLA

Top each potato with 6 ounces (170 g) plain or vanilla nondairy yogurt, ½ cup (120 ml) Maple Cinnamon Granola Clusters (see page 61), a pinch of cinnamon, and a drizzle of maple syrup.

BREAKFAST SWEET POTATOES WITH HUMMUS, CHICKPEAS, AND GREENS

Top each potato with ¼ cup (60 ml) Smoked Paprika Hummus (see page 149) or any other hummus, ⅓ cup (about 60 g) cooked beans or lentils, and a handful of steamed greens or steamed broccoli florets. A drizzle of Everyday Lemon Tahini Dressing (see page 66) is a nice extra touch.

MAPLE CINNAMON GRANOLA

There are two types of granola people: those who like granola to be fine, sort of like cereal, and those who are all about clusters. I'm a cluster girl, and I've designed my go-to granola recipe accordingly, using brown rice syrup to achieve a clumpy texture and baking the granola low and slow. Paired with fresh fruit and nondairy yogurt, the homemade clusters make for a terrific breakfast that comes together quickly. Note that the recipe for the granola makes more than is needed for these bowls. That isn't a problem! It keeps well in an airtight container stored in a cool place for a couple of weeks, so you'll be one step ahead on busy mornings.

MAKES 7 TO 8 CUPS (760 G) GRANOLA, ENOUGH FOR 4 BOWLS AND LEFTOVERS

MAPLE CINNAMON GRANOLA CLUSTERS

3 cups (270 g) rolled oats

¼ cup oat bran (25 g) or toasted wheat germ (30 g)

1 cup (140 g) pumpkin seeds or sunflower seeds

1 cup (about 100 g) sliced or slivered almonds or chopped walnuts, pecans, or pistachios

¼ cup (60 ml) olive oil

½ cup (120 ml) brown rice syrup or maple syrup

1 teaspoon vanilla extract

¾ teaspoon salt

½ teaspoon ground cinnamon

¼ teaspoon ground cardamom (optional)

1 cup (about 120 g) dried cherries or cranberries, or 1 cup (145 g) raisins or chopped dried apricots

BOWLS

24 ounces (680 g) plain or vanilla nondairy yogurt

4 cups (600 g) fresh fruit, such as berries, sliced bananas, or chopped apples, pears, peaches, or plums

To make the granola clusters, preheat the oven to 325°F (165°C) and line two rimmed baking sheets with parchment paper.

Combine the oats, oat bran, pumpkin seeds, and almonds in a large bowl. In a small bowl or measuring cup, whisk together the oil, brown rice syrup, vanilla, salt, cinnamon, and cardamom. Add to the oat mixture and stir until well combined.

Spread the oat mixture on the lined baking sheets in an even layer. Bake for 30 to 35 minutes without stirring, until the edges are browning and the center is lightly golden.

Let cool completely on the baking sheets, then break the granola into clusters. Add the dried fruit and mix gently.

To serve, divide the yogurt among four bowls. Top each with ½ cup (120 ml) of the granola and 1 cup (150 g) of the fruit.

SALADS

Veganism has opened my eyes to how diverse and satisfying salads can be. My favorite salad recipes aren't dainty piles of greens that live on appetizer plates; they're big, bold, abundant dishes, hearty enough to fill a pasta bowl.

Early in my blogging years, I wrote a post titled "How to Build a Meal-Sized Salad." The post was just what it sounds like: a primer on making everyday salads more filling. Not surprisingly, the main piece of advice I offered was that salads should always include protein, complex carbs, and healthful fat. It's still one of the most popular posts on my blog—a sign that people crave hearty salad recipes that can hold their own as meals.

The eighteen salads in this chapter pick up where that blog post left off. These are salads that you can bring to potlucks or family gatherings, confident that they'll leave no one hungry. Many of the recipes are more heavily populated by legumes, grains, and nuts than they are by greens, and that's the point: they're vegetable-centric, but vegetables don't steal the show. Instead, they graciously cohabitate with heartier ingredients, ensuring that no macronutrient is left behind.

These recipes also challenge the notion that salad is a dish best served cold. Many of them are fine to serve warm or at room temperature, especially the Masala Lentil Salad with Cumin-Roasted Carrots (page 74), the Roasted Kabocha Salad with Barley and Lemon Miso Vinaigrette (page 78), and the Zucchini Pesto Pasta Salad (page 82). The Warm Tofu Chop Salad with Peanut Dressing (page 81) features both hot and cold ingredients, and that temperature contrast is part of what makes the salad so intriguing. Warm salads like these are an especially good vehicle for enjoying vegetables and greens in the winter, when a cold meal is less than appealing.

For some of the lighter salads, like the Charred Broccoli Salad with Freekeh and Spring Herbs (page 70), the Guacamole Quinoa Salad with Black Beans (page 73), or the Tuscan Kale Salad with White Beans (page 89), it's a smart idea to allow cooked grains or beans to cool to room temperature before mixing, so that the ingredients taste fresh and crisp.

WILD RICE SALAD
WITH CHERRY TOMATOES, CORN, GREEN BEANS, AND TOFU

Pan-cooked cherry tomatoes, heated until they burst, are one of my favorite ways to add concentrated flavor to summer recipes. Their sweet juices infuse other ingredients, so the rest of the dish can be simple. This bright, colorful salad is a perfect example of what burst tomatoes can do. If you're short on time, you can substitute quinoa, bulgur, or another quick-cooking grain for the wild rice.

MAKES 4 SERVINGS

1 cup (160 g) wild rice

7 ounces (200 g) green beans, trimmed and cut into 1-inch (2.5-cm) pieces

1½ cups (235 g) fresh or frozen corn kernels

2 tablespoons olive oil

3 cloves garlic, thinly sliced

10 ounces (285 g) cherry tomatoes

Salt

8 ounces (225 g) smoked or baked tofu, cut into small cubes

3 cups (90 g) firmly packed mesclun, baby romaine, or baby arugula

1 small shallot, finely chopped

1 tablespoon freshly squeezed lemon juice

¼ cup (10 g) chopped fresh basil leaves

Freshly ground black pepper

Cook the wild rice as directed on page 14.

Meanwhile, bring a medium pot of water to a boil. Add the green beans and corn and blanch for about 2 minutes, until the beans are bright green and crisp-tender. Drain immediately.

Heat 1 tablespoon of the oil in a medium skillet over medium heat. When the oil is glistening, add the garlic and cherry tomatoes, along with a pinch of salt. Cook, stirring occasionally, for 6 to 7 minutes, until the tomatoes are bursting and releasing their juices. Remove from the heat and discard the garlic.

Transfer the tomatoes to a large bowl. Add the wild rice, green beans, corn, tofu, mesclun, and shallot and toss gently to combine. Drizzle with the remaining 1 tablespoon oil and the lemon juice and scatter the basil over the top. Toss again, then taste and adjust the seasonings if desired. Serve warm or at room temperature (though chilled leftovers are nice, too!).

ROASTED CAULIFLOWER SALAD
WITH LENTILS

MAKES 4 SERVINGS OF SALAD,
AND ⅔ TO ¾ CUP (160 TO 175 ML)
OF DRESSING

SALAD

1 medium cauliflower, chopped
into small pieces

2 tablespoons olive oil

1 tablespoon finely grated
lemon zest

1 tablespoon ground sumac
(optional)

2 teaspoons ground cumin

½ teaspoon coarse salt

¼ teaspoon freshly ground
black pepper

⅔ cup (135 g) dried brown or
green lentils, or 1 (15-oz, or 425-g)
can lentils, drained and rinsed

2 cups (60 g) firmly packed baby
arugula

½ small bunch kale, stemmed
and finely chopped

2 carrots, peeled and grated

**EVERYDAY LEMON TAHINI
DRESSING**

¼ cup (60 ml) warm water, plus
more if desired

¼ cup (60 g) tahini

1 clove garlic, finely minced
or grated

2 tablespoons freshly squeezed
lemon juice

½ teaspoon agave nectar
or maple syrup

¼ teaspoon salt

⅛ teaspoon freshly ground
black pepper

The lemony flavor of sumac, a tart Middle Eastern spice, brightens up roasted vegetables without being heavy-handed. In this salad, it's used as a spice rub for tender roasted cauliflower, which is then tossed with lentils, arugula, and crunchy carrots. Sumac can be found in Middle Eastern markets or online; if you can't get your hands on it, you'll still get a kick of citrus from lemon zest and the Everyday Lemon Tahini Dressing, which is aptly named because I use it so often. You'll discover that it makes many appearances in these pages!

To make the salad, preheat the oven to 400°F (200°C) and line a rimmed baking sheet with parchment paper. In a large bowl, toss the cauliflower with the oil until evenly coated. Sprinkle with the lemon zest, sumac, cumin, salt, and pepper and toss again. Bake for 30 minutes, until the edges of the cauliflower are beginning to brown and crisp, stirring once halfway through the baking time.

Meanwhile, cook the lentils as directed on page 15. Drain, rinse under cold running water, then let drain completely. (If you're using canned lentils, you can skip this step.)

Put the arugula, kale, and carrots in a large bowl.

To make the dressing, combine all the ingredients in a small bowl or measuring cup and whisk until evenly blended. If the dressing is thicker than you'd like, whisk in water by the tablespoonful to achieve the desired consistency. (Stored in an airtight container in the refrigerator, the dressing will keep for 1 week.)

Pour half of the dressing over the arugula mixture and use your hands to massage it into the vegetables until they've softened. Add the cauliflower, the lentils, and the rest of the dressing and toss gently until well combined. Serve right away.

SWEET POTATO SALAD
WITH TEMPEH AND MAPLE MUSTARD DRESSING

The sweet, salty maple mustard dressing featured in this autumn salad is one of my all-time favorites. It began as a vinaigrette, but one of my recipe testers tried it with tahini in place of the oil and couldn't stop raving about the results. When I tried her version, which is creamier and denser, I could see why she loved it so much. I use both versions often, and both are well-suited to this salad of roasted sweet potatoes, earthy tempeh, and peppery greens.

———————————————

To make the salad, put the tempeh in a shallow glass bowl or container, preferably one large enough to fit all of the tempeh in a single layer. In a small bowl or measuring cup, whisk together the tamari, vinegar, maple syrup, and paprika. Pour the mixture over the tempeh and stir gently to evenly coat the cubes. Cover and refrigerate for at least 1 hour and up to 12 hours.

Preheat the oven to 400°F (200°C) and line two rimmed baking sheets with parchment paper. In a large bowl, toss the sweet potatoes with the oil until evenly coated. Transfer to one of the lined baking sheets and sprinkle generously with salt and pepper. Bake for 30 to 35 minutes, until fork-tender and starting to brown.

Meanwhile, drain the tempeh and spread it on the other lined baking sheet. Bake for 15 minutes, until the tempeh is beginning to brown.

Transfer the sweet potatoes and tempeh to a large bowl and let cool for about 10 minutes. Add the arugula.

To make the dressing, combine the oil, maple syrup, mustard, tamari, apple cider vinegar, balsamic vinegar, and nutritional yeast in a small bowl or measuring cup. Whisk to combine. If the dressing is thicker than you'd like, whisk in the warm water as needed. (Stored in an airtight container in the refrigerator, the dressing will keep for 1 week.)

Pour the dressing over the salad and toss gently to combine. Fold in any additional toppings and serve.

MAKES 3 TO 4 SERVINGS OF SALAD, AND ABOUT ½ CUP (120 ML) OF DRESSING

SALAD

8 ounces (225 g) tempeh, cut into ½-inch (1.3-cm) cubes

2 tablespoons tamari or Bragg Liquid Aminos

2 tablespoons apple cider vinegar

1 tablespoon maple syrup

¼ teaspoon smoked paprika

2 medium sweet potatoes, peeled and cut into ½-inch (1.3-cm) cubes

1 tablespoon olive oil

Coarse salt and freshly ground black pepper

5 cups (150 g) firmly packed baby arugula

¼ cup (10 g) snipped fresh chives or chopped scallions, green parts only

MAPLE MUSTARD DRESSING

2 tablespoons olive oil or tahini

1 tablespoon maple syrup

1 tablespoon Dijon mustard

1 tablespoon tamari or Bragg Liquid Aminos

1 tablespoon apple cider vinegar

1 tablespoon balsamic vinegar

1½ tablespoons nutritional yeast

1 to 2 tablespoons warm water, if needed

OPTIONAL TOPPINGS

Snipped fresh chives, toasted sunflower or pumpkin seeds

CHARRED BROCCOLI SALAD
WITH FREEKEH AND SPRING HERBS

Roasting broccoli until it's crisp and browning at the edges brings out a pleasantly smoky flavor. Charred broccoli makes a great addition to cooked grains, but it's especially interesting when contrasted with fresh herbs and tender greens, as in this springtime salad. The nutty flavor of cracked freekeh adds even more complexity, but if you can't find freekeh, bulgur wheat and quinoa are both great substitutes.

MAKES 4 SERVINGS OF SALAD, AND ABOUT ⅓ CUP (80 ML) OF DRESSING

SALAD

1 pound (450 g) broccoli

1 tablespoon neutral vegetable oil

Coarse salt and freshly ground black pepper

½ cup (100 g) cracked freekeh

1½ cups (270 g) cooked navy beans, or 1 (15-oz, or 425-g) can, drained and rinsed

¼ cup (10 g) chopped fresh parsley

2 tablespoons chopped fresh tarragon leaves

4 cups (120 g) firmly packed baby arugula

DRESSING

3 tablespoons olive oil

2 tablespoons freshly squeezed lemon juice

½ teaspoon Dijon mustard

1 tablespoon finely chopped shallot

¼ teaspoon salt

Generous pinch of freshly ground black pepper

To make the salad, preheat the oven to 475°F (245°C) and line a rimmed baking sheet with parchment paper. Trim and peel the broccoli stems. Slice the stems into rounds about ½ inch (1.3 cm) thick and cut the tops into small florets. In a large bowl, toss the broccoli with the oil until evenly coated. Spread it on the lined baking sheet and sprinkle with salt and pepper. Bake for about 30 minutes, until the florets are slightly charred and the edges of the stems are browning, stirring once halfway through the baking time.

Meanwhile, cook the freekeh as directed on page 13. Transfer to a large bowl. Add the broccoli and let cool for about 10 minutes. Add the beans, parsley, tarragon, and arugula.

To make the dressing, combine all the ingredients in a small bowl or measuring cup and whisk until evenly blended.

Gently toss the salad ingredients, then pour in the dressing and toss again until evenly coated. Taste and adjust the seasonings if desired. Serve at room temperature.

GUACAMOLE QUINOA SALAD
WITH BLACK BEANS

This is basically a big batch of guacamole, dressed up as salad! You start by mixing chopped and roughly mashed avocado with lime, salt, onion, and cilantro—just as if you were throwing together a bowl of fresh guac—then you fold in protein-rich quinoa and black beans. It's a fast and easy dish to make if the quinoa is cooked ahead of time, which makes it perfect for last-minute summer lunches.

MAKES 4 SERVINGS

1 cup (170 g) quinoa, rinsed

2 Hass avocados, halved, pitted, and peeled

½ teaspoon coarse salt

2 tablespoons freshly squeezed lime juice, plus more if desired

½ small white or red onion, finely diced

½ cup (10 g) loosely packed, chopped fresh cilantro

1 cup (150 g) cherry tomatoes, quartered

1½ cups (170 g) cooked black beans, or 1 (15-oz, or 425-g) can, drained and rinsed

Olive oil (optional), for drizzling

Chopped romaine lettuce or whole romaine lettuce leaves, for serving

OPTIONAL TOPPINGS

Finely minced garlic, hot sauce, red pepper flakes

Cook the quinoa as directed on page 13. Allow quinoa to cool to room temperature, about 30 minutes.

Score the avocado flesh (still in the skins) with a paring knife, then scoop the flesh into a large bowl. Coarsely mash about half of the avocado with a fork, leaving plenty of chunks intact. Add the salt, lime juice, onion, and cilantro and mix well.

Add the tomatoes, black beans, and quinoa and stir gently until fully incorporated. Fold in any additional toppings and add a drizzle of olive oil. Taste and adjust the seasonings if desired; you may want to add a bit more salt or lime juice. Serve on a bed of chopped romaine lettuce or stuffed into whole romaine leaves.

MASALA LENTIL SALAD
WITH CUMIN-ROASTED CARROTS

When I first whisked together the dressing for this recipe, I worried that the garam masala would overwhelm the salad, but it doesn't; instead, the sweet notes of the Indian spice blend are perfectly balanced by the garlic, ginger, and a bright splash of apple cider vinegar. I add a generous handful of mint to the dish to contrast with the earthiness of the lentils and roasted carrots. The pomegranate molasses isn't necessary if you don't have it on hand, but if you do, it's a wonderful way to add a sweet-and-sour finish to the dish.

———————————————————

To make the salad, preheat the oven to 400°F (200°C) and line a rimmed baking sheet with parchment paper. Put the carrots in a large bowl. Drizzle with the oil and maple syrup, sprinkle with the cumin, and toss until evenly coated. Transfer to the lined baking sheet, spreading them in a single layer (you may need a second baking sheet). Season generously with coarse salt and pepper. Bake for about 40 minutes, until the carrots are fork-tender and browning.

Meanwhile, cook the lentils as directed on page 15. Drain, rinse under cold running water, then let drain completely. (If you're using canned lentils, you can skip this step.)

Put the carrots and lentils in a large bowl and let cool for 10 minutes. Add the onion, arugula, and mint.

To make the dressing, combine all the ingredients in a small bowl or measuring cup and whisk until evenly combined.

Pour the dressing over the salad and toss gently until evenly combined. Taste and adjust the seasonings if desired. Drizzle with about 1 tablespoon pomegranate molasses, and offer the toasted seeds on the side.

MAKES 4 TO 5 SERVINGS OF SALAD, AND ABOUT ⅓ CUP (80 ML) OF DRESSING

SALAD

1½ pounds (680 g) carrots, peeled and sliced into ½-inch (1.3-cm) rounds

2 tablespoons neutral vegetable oil

1 tablespoon maple syrup

1½ teaspoons ground cumin

Coarse salt and freshly ground black pepper

1 cup (200 g) dried beluga or French green lentils, or 2 (15-oz, or 425-g) cans lentils, drained and rinsed

½ red onion, finely chopped

2 cups (60 g) firmly packed baby arugula, mizuna, or baby kale

⅓ cup (13 g) chopped fresh mint leaves

DRESSING

3 tablespoons olive oil

1 clove garlic, pressed or finely grated

1 teaspoon minced or finely grated ginger

1 teaspoon garam masala

2 tablespoons apple cider vinegar

½ teaspoon salt

Freshly ground black pepper

OPTIONAL TOPPINGS

Pomegranate molasses; toasted pumpkin seeds, sunflower seeds, or pine nuts

SPRING PANZANELLA
WITH ARTICHOKES, ASPARAGUS, PEAS, AND LEMON DILL VINAIGRETTE

I'm devoted to using whole grains in my salads, but sometimes bread and only bread will do. That's when panzanella, an Italian bread-based salad, hits the spot. This panzanella is full of contrast: rustic pieces of toasted bread meet light spring greens and tender sweet peas. It's an easy salad to throw together at the last moment and enjoy for an impromptu lunch. The dressing is a simple vinaigrette enhanced with finely chopped dill for a fresh touch.

MAKES 4 SERVINGS OF SALAD, AND ABOUT ½ CUP (120 ML) OF VINAIGRETTE

SALAD

1 bunch asparagus, trimmed and cut into 1-inch (2.5-cm) pieces

1 cup (140 g) fresh or frozen green peas

4 to 5 cups (120 to 150 g) firmly packed mesclun or baby arugula

1 (6-oz, or 170-g) jar marinated artichoke hearts, drained and chopped

1½ cups (250 g) cooked chickpeas, or 1 (15-oz, or 425-g) can, drained and rinsed

4 slices whole grain bread, preferably whole wheat sourdough, toasted and cubed

VINAIGRETTE

5 tablespoons (75 ml) olive oil

2 heaping tablespoons finely chopped fresh dill, or 2 teaspoons dried dill weed

1 scant teaspoon Dijon mustard

2 tablespoons freshly squeezed lemon juice

¼ teaspoon salt

Freshly ground black pepper

To make the salad, bring a medium pot of water to a boil. Add the asparagus and blanch for 2 to 3 minutes (less if the spears are very thin), until just tender. Add the peas and blanch for 1 to 2 minutes, until the peas are bright green. Drain immediately.

Put the greens, artichoke hearts, chickpeas, and bread cubes in a large bowl.

To make the vinaigrette, combine all the ingredients in a small bowl or measuring cup and whisk until evenly blended.

Pat the asparagus and peas dry with a paper towel and add to the greens. Toss gently, then pour in the dressing and toss again until well combined. Taste and adjust the seasonings if desired. Serve right away.

ROASTED KABOCHA SALAD
WITH BARLEY AND LEMON MISO VINAIGRETTE

I try to resist picking favorites in the vegetable kingdom, but I do think kabocha squash reigns supreme over all the other winter squashes. This is thanks to its deep flavor and firm, buttery texture—a little lighter than sweet potato, but richer than most squashes. It takes a starring role in this salad, a wonderfully earthy mixture that's enlivened by a bright lemon miso dressing.

MAKES 4 SERVINGS OF SALAD, AND ABOUT ½ CUP (120 ML) OF VINAIGRETTE

SALAD

1 pound (450 g) kabocha squash, seeded and cut into 1-inch (2.5-cm) cubes

1 red onion, cut into wedges

1 tablespoon tamari

1 tablespoon neutral vegetable oil

Red pepper flakes

¾ cup (150 g) pearl barley

1 small head radicchio, torn into bite-size pieces

4 cups (120 g) firmly packed mizuna, baby arugula, or baby kale

¼ cup (35 g) toasted pumpkin seeds

VINAIGRETTE

2 tablespoons white miso

2 tablespoons freshly squeezed lemon juice

1 teaspoon Dijon mustard

1 teaspoon maple syrup

¼ cup (60 ml) neutral vegetable oil

1 scallion, white and green parts, chopped

Pinch of red pepper flakes

To make the salad, preheat the oven to 400°F (200°C) and line a rimmed baking sheet with parchment paper. Put the squash and onion in a large bowl. Whisk together the tamari and oil, drizzle over the vegetables, and toss until the vegetables are evenly coated. Spread evenly on the lined baking sheet and bake for about 30 minutes, until the squash is tender.

Meanwhile, cook the barley as directed on page 12.

Transfer the roasted vegetables and barley to a large bowl and let cool for about 10 minutes. Add the radicchio, mizuna, and pumpkin seeds.

To make the vinaigrette, combine the miso and lemon juice in a small bowl or measuring cup and whisk to create a thick slurry. Whisk in the mustard, maple syrup, and oil until evenly combined. Stir in the scallion and red pepper flakes.

Gently toss the salad, then pour in half of the dressing and toss again. Add additional dressing if needed to coat the salad well. Serve right away.

WARM TOFU CHOP SALAD
WITH PEANUT DRESSING

This dish—a sort of hybrid between salad and stir-fry—was inspired by Sara Forte, the cookbook author and ingenious blogger behind *Sprouted Kitchen*. Her tofu chop salad got me thinking about ways to combine warm tofu with cold, crunchy veggies for a quick meal. I like to top the dish with a creamy peanut sauce that's equally good for dipping spring rolls, drizzling onto bowls, or (let's be honest) sneaking by the spoonful.

MAKES 4 SERVINGS OF SALAD, AND ABOUT ⅔ CUP (160 ML) OF DRESSING

SALAD

¾ cup (150 g) short-grain brown rice

1½ cups (100 g) snow peas

1 tablespoon neutral vegetable oil

1 (15-oz, or 425-g) block extra-firm tofu, preferably pressed (see page 15), cut into ¾-inch (2-cm) cubes

3 cups (90 g) firmly packed baby spinach

3 tablespoons water

Tamari, for seasoning

3 carrots, shredded or cut into thin strips with a julienne peeler

1 red or yellow bell pepper, chopped

DRESSING

¼ cup (60 g) smooth peanut butter

1½ tablespoons tamari

2 teaspoons agave nectar or maple syrup

1 tablespoon rice vinegar

1 teaspoon toasted sesame oil

1 clove garlic, minced or finely grated

2 teaspoons minced or finely grated fresh ginger

3 tablespoons hot water

OPTIONAL TOPPINGS

Sriracha sauce, lime wedges, chopped scallions, chopped fresh cilantro, chopped roasted peanuts, black or white sesame seeds

To make the salad, cook the brown rice as directed on page 13.

Meanwhile, bring a medium pot of water to boil. Add the snow peas and blanch for about 2 minutes, until bright green and crisp-tender. Drain immediately and let cool for a few minutes, then coarsely chop if desired.

Heat the sesame oil in a medium nonstick skillet over medium-high heat. Add the tofu and cook, stirring frequently, for 6 to 8 minutes, until lightly browned. Add the spinach and water and cook, stirring constantly, for about 2 minutes, until the spinach is just wilted. Stir in a splash of tamari.

Transfer the tofu mixture to a large bowl. Add the rice and let cool for about 10 minutes. Add the snow peas, carrots, and bell pepper.

To make the dressing, combine all the ingredients in a small bowl and whisk until evenly combined.

Pour the dressing over the salad and toss gently to combine. Serve with toppings of choice.

ZUCCHINI PESTO PASTA SALAD

This simple, summery pasta salad can be served either warm or cool. The flavors will intensify once the salad has had a chance to sit for a few hours in the fridge, so you can count on it for great leftovers or as a make-ahead option for gatherings. The dish gets bonus points for its flexibility, too: roasted broccoli, eggplant, or cauliflower can be substituted for the zucchini in the summertime. In the cooler months, you can create a seasonal variation by substituting acorn or butternut squash and a kale or sage pesto.

_____

MAKES 4 SERVINGS OF SALAD, AND ABOUT 1 CUP (240 ML) OF PESTO

SALAD

3 medium zucchini or summer squashes, halved lengthwise and then cut crosswise into ½-inch (1.3-cm) half-moons

1 tablespoon olive oil

Coarse salt and freshly ground black pepper

8 ounces (225 g) penne or rotini pasta

1½ cups (270 g) cooked navy, Great Northern, or cannellini beans, or 1 (15-oz, 425-g) can, drained and rinsed

PESTO

2½ cups (50 g) loosely packed fresh basil leaves

1 clove garlic, chopped

¼ cup (25 g) walnuts

3 tablespoons nutritional yeast

¼ cup (60 ml) olive oil

1 tablespoon freshly squeezed lemon juice

½ teaspoon salt

Freshly ground black pepper

OPTIONAL ACCOMPANIMENTS

Arugula, baby spinach, or other tender leafy green; lemon wedges; Cheesy Hemp Seed Topping (see page 89) or vegan parmesan

To make the salad, preheat the oven to 400°F (200°C) and line a rimmed baking sheet with parchment paper. In a large bowl, toss the zucchini with the oil until evenly coated. Season with salt and pepper and toss again. Spread evenly on the lined baking sheet and bake for 25 to 30 minutes, until tender and lightly browned.

Meanwhile, bring a large pot of salted water to boil. Stir in the pasta, then adjust the heat to maintain a low boil. Cook, stirring occasionally, until the pasta is tender but still firm. Drain well.

Put the pasta, zucchini, and beans in a large bowl and stir gently to combine.

To make the pesto, combine the basil, garlic, walnuts, nutritional yeast, oil, lemon juice, and salt in a food processor and process for 1 minute. Scrape down the sides of the work bowl, season with pepper to taste, then process for 30 seconds, until the pesto has a mostly smooth, even consistency.

Add the pesto to the pasta mixture and stir gently to combine. Serve warm, cool, or at room temperature, scooped over fresh greens, and with your favorite toppings.

WINTER SALAD
WITH BULGUR, RADICCHIO, AND TOASTED ALMONDS

The more limited produce offerings of colder months encourage me to get creative with salads. In place of fresh greens, I'll often use a base of radicchio, chicory, endive, or even thinly shaved root vegetables. I brighten up dressings with citrus zest, parsley, or flavored oils and vinegars, which offer a nice contrast to the earthiness of winter vegetables. Walnut and hazelnut oil are my favorites: they're pricey but intensely flavorful, so a small amount goes a long way.

MAKES 4 SERVINGS OF SALAD, AND ABOUT ½ CUP (120 ML) OF VINAIGRETTE

SALAD

¾ cup (135 g) bulgur wheat

⅓ cup (about 35 g) sliced or slivered almonds

1 head radicchio (about 8 ounces, or 225 g), torn into bite-size pieces

1½ cups (250 g) cooked chickpeas, or 1 (15-oz, or 425-g) can chickpeas, drained and rinsed

⅓ cup (50 g) golden raisins

¼ cup (10 g) chopped fresh parsley

VINAIGRETTE

2 tablespoons olive oil

2 tablespoons walnut oil, hazelnut oil, or additional olive oil

1 tablespoon finely grated lemon zest

1 tablespoon freshly squeezed lemon juice, plus more as needed

1 tablespoon sherry or red wine vinegar (more as needed)

1 teaspoon maple syrup

1 small clove garlic, minced or finely grated

½ teaspoon salt

Pinch of freshly ground black pepper

To make the salad, cook the bulgur as directed on page 13.

Meanwhile, put the almonds in a small skillet and toast over medium heat, shaking or stirring frequently, until just golden; they'll keep cooking after you remove them from the heat, so it's better to stop too soon rather than too late.

Put the bulgur in a large bowl and let cool briefly. Add the almonds, radicchio, chickpeas, raisins, and parsley.

To make the vinaigrette, combine all the ingredients in a small bowl or measuring cup and whisk until evenly combined.

Pour the vinaigrette over the salad and toss well. Taste and adjust the seasonings if desired. Serve warm or at room temperature.

SESAME CITRUS SOBA SALAD

The citrus in this recipe—a combination of orange and lime—adds brightness without being overly sweet or tart. It's a perfect contrast to the bold flavors of garlic, ginger, and tamari, not to mention the earthiness of buckwheat noodles. The salad is easy to pull together for a casual lunch or light dinner. To make the dish even more substantial, you can add marinated and baked tofu cubes, or you can serve it bowl-style, with extra steamed vegetables.

MAKES 4 SERVINGS OF SALAD, AND ABOUT 1 CUP (240 ML) OF DRESSING

SALAD

8 ounces (225 g) soba noodles

1½ cups (225 g) shelled edamame, steamed

3 carrots, grated or cut into matchsticks

1½ cups (105 g) shredded red cabbage

2 scallions, green parts only, chopped

½ cup (15 g) chopped fresh cilantro

DRESSING

⅓ cup (85 g) almond butter or tahini

1 tablespoon finely grated orange zest

6 tablespoons (90 ml) freshly squeezed orange juice

2 tablespoons freshly squeezed lime juice

1½ tablespoons tamari

1 to 2 cloves garlic, minced or finely grated

1 tablespoon minced or finely grated ginger, or 1 teaspoon ground ginger

1 teaspoon toasted sesame oil

Pinch of red pepper flakes

OPTIONAL TOPPINGS

Cubed baked tofu, sriracha sauce, chopped scallions, red pepper flakes

To make the salad, bring a large pot of salted water to a boil over high heat. Add the soba noodles, then adjust the heat to maintain a low boil. Cook, stirring occasionally, until the noodles are just softening to al dente. Add the edamame and boil for another 2 minutes. Drain and rinse under cold running water.

Put the carrots, cabbage, scallions, and cilantro in a large bowl.

To make the dressing, combine all the ingredients in a small bowl and whisk until well blended.

To assemble the salad, add the soba and edamame to the vegetables and toss gently. Then pour in the dressing and toss again until well combined. Taste and adjust the seasonings if desired. Serve at room temperature, with toppings of choice.

TUSCAN KALE SALAD
WITH WHITE BEANS

I've made and enjoyed countless kale salads, but this one has become my go-to for sharing with friends. Lacinato kale is sometimes called Tuscan kale because of its popularity in central and northern Italian cooking, and in keeping with that theme, the salad also features cannellini beans, farro, and my Cheesy Hemp Seed Topping—an awesome, all-purpose, homemade spin on parmesan. This recipe yields more of the hemp seed topping than you'll need for the salad. Just store any leftovers in an airtight container in the refrigerator; it will keep for a week or so, and then you'll have it on hand for sprinkling on bowls and pastas. You can also replace it with your favorite store-bought vegan parmesan.

MAKES 4 SERVINGS OF SALAD, AND ABOUT ⅔ CUP (160 ML) OF HEMP SEED TOPPING

SALAD

⅔ cup (135 g) farro (pearl or hulled)

¼ cup (60 ml) olive oil

2 tablespoons freshly squeezed lemon juice

½ teaspoon Dijon mustard

1 clove garlic, minced or finely grated

¼ teaspoon salt

Freshly ground black pepper

1 bunch Lacinato kale, stemmed and cut into thin strips

¼ cup (35 g) golden raisins

1½ cups (270 g) cooked cannellini or Great Northern beans, or 1 (15-oz, or 425-g) can, drained and rinsed

CHEESY HEMP SEED TOPPING

⅓ cup (25 g) nutritional yeast

⅓ cup (55 g) shelled hemp seeds

¼ teaspoon salt

½ teaspoon olive oil

To make the salad, cook the farro as directed on page 13. Rinse the farro under cool running water and allow it to drain.

In a small bowl or measuring cup, combine the oil, lemon juice, mustard, garlic, salt, and a generous grinding of pepper and whisk until well blended.

Put the kale in a large bowl. Pour in half of the dressing and use your hands to massage it into the kale until it's softened. Add the farro, raisins, and white beans and stir gently to combine. Pour in the rest of the dressing and stir again.

To make the hemp seed topping, combine the nutritional yeast, hemp seeds, and salt in a food processor and process for about 15 seconds. Add the oil and pulse for 10 seconds. Sprinkle 3 to 4 tablespoons of the mixture over the salad and stir gently to combine. Taste and adjust the seasonings if desired. Serve at room temperature.

BUTTERNUT SQUASH SALAD
WITH RED QUINOA AND PUMPKIN SEEDS

As anyone who has read my blog knows, I have a weakness for sweet and savory flavor combinations. This salad delivers both, with further contrast from the base of peppery, bitter arugula. It's a perfect dish to bring to Thanksgiving or another winter holiday.

MAKES 4 TO 6 SERVINGS

1½ pounds (680 g) butternut squash, peeled, seeded, and cubed

1 tablespoon neutral vegetable oil

Salt and freshly ground black pepper

1 cup (170 g) red quinoa, rinsed

⅓ cup (45 g) raw or toasted pumpkin seeds

⅓ cup (40 g) dried cranberries

3 cups (90 g) firmly packed baby arugula

¼ cup (60 ml) olive oil

1 tablespoon freshly squeezed lemon juice

1 tablespoon apple cider vinegar, sherry vinegar, or champagne vinegar

1 teaspoon maple syrup

1 small shallot, minced

Preheat the oven to 400°F (200°C) and line a rimmed baking sheet with parchment paper. In a large bowl, toss the squash with the oil until evenly coated. Spread the squash in a single layer on the lined baking sheet and sprinkle generously with salt and pepper. Bake for 30 to 40 minutes, until the squash is fork-tender, stirring once halfway through the baking time.

Meanwhile, cook the quinoa as directed on page 13.

Put the squash and quinoa in a large bowl and let cool for about 10 minutes. Add the pumpkin seeds, cranberries, and arugula.

In a small bowl or measuring cup, combine the oil, lemon juice, vinegar, maple syrup, ½ teaspoon salt, and a pinch of pepper and whisk until evenly combined. Stir in the shallot.

Gently toss the squash mixture. Pour in the dressing and toss again. Taste and adjust the seasonings if desired. Serve right away.

VIETNAMESE RICE NOODLE SALAD
WITH SEARED TOFU

MAKES 4 SERVINGS OF SALAD,
AND ABOUT ⅔ CUP (160 ML)
OF DRESSING

DRESSING

3 tablespoons freshly squeezed
lime juice

2 tablespoons rice vinegar

2 tablespoons tamari

1 to 2 cloves garlic, finely minced
or grated

1 teaspoon finely grated or minced
fresh ginger

2 tablespoons sugar

2 Thai chiles, finely chopped

SALAD

1 small bunch curly kale, stemmed
and finely chopped

1 tablespoon olive oil

2 teaspoons freshly squeezed
lime juice

2 teaspoons neutral vegetable oil

1 (14-oz, or 400-g) block extra-firm
tofu, preferably pressed (see
page 15), cut into 1-inch
(2.5-cm) cubes

8 ounces (225 g) rice vermicelli
noodles

1 large cucumber, peeled and cut
into matchsticks or sliced into long
strips using a julienne peeler

1 red or yellow bell pepper, cut
into matchsticks

1½ cups (165 g) grated carrots
(about 3 carrots)

⅓ cup (50 g) chopped peanuts

¼ cup (10 g) chopped fresh
mint leaves

⅓ cup (13 g) chopped fresh
basil leaves

Red pepper flakes

Sriracha sauce (optional),
for serving

This salad is perfect for hot, lazy summer nights. Aside from searing the tofu, there's not much cooking to do, yet the dish is vibrant and filling. I recommend whisking the dressing together in advance—up to 3 days ahead of time—so that the garlic and ginger can mingle a bit. Be sure to chill the salad before you serve.

To make the dressing, combine all the ingredients in a small bowl and whisk until evenly blended.

To make the salad, put the kale in a large bowl. Add the olive oil and lime juice and use your hands to massage the oil and lime juice into the kale; it will soften and decrease in volume.

Heat the vegetable oil in a medium nonstick skillet over medium-high heat. Add the tofu and cook, stirring frequently, for 6 to 8 minutes, until lightly browned.

Bring a large pot of salted water to a boil over high heat. Add the vermicelli, then adjust the heat to maintain a low boil. Cook, stirring occasionally, until the noodles are tender but still firm (about 5 minutes). Drain and rinse the cooked noodles under cold, running water, then drain well. Use a knife or kitchen shears to cut the noodles a few times (this will make it easier to mix the salad).

Add the noodles to the kale, along with the tofu, cucumber, bell pepper, carrots, and peanuts and stir gently. Whisk the dressing, then pour it over the salad and toss gently until thoroughly combined. Add the mint and basil, season with red pepper flakes, and toss again. Refrigerate for at least 1 hour before serving. Serve with a squeeze of sriracha.

TEMPEH

8 ounces (225 g) tempeh, cut into
¾-inch (2-cm) cubes

¼ cup (60 ml) freshly squeezed
lemon juice

2 tablespoons tamari

1 teaspoon Dijon mustard

2 teaspoons agave nectar or
maple syrup

¼ teaspoon freshly ground black
pepper, plus more for dusting

1 tablespoon olive oil

CROUTONS

4 slices whole grain bread, cut
into 1-inch (2.5-cm) cubes

2 tablespoons olive oil

½ to 1 teaspoon garlic powder

Coarse salt

CAESAR DRESSING

¾ cup (95 g) raw cashews, soaked
for at least 2 hours and drained

½ cup (120 ml) water

1 teaspoon Dijon mustard

2 cloves garlic, coarsely chopped

2 tablespoons capers

1½ tablespoons freshly squeezed
lemon juice

1½ tablespoons red wine vinegar

½ teaspoon salt

¼ teaspoon freshly ground black
pepper

¼ cup (20 g) nutritional yeast

1 small bunch Lacinato kale,
stemmed and cut into thin strips

5 cups (150 g) firmly packed,
chopped romaine lettuce

⅓ cup chopped sun-dried
tomatoes, oil-packed (40 g)
or dry-packed (20 g)

PROTEIN-PACKED CAESAR

Everything about this Caesar salad, from the tangy sun-dried
tomatoes to the egg-free dressing to the baked tempeh, is
nontraditional. Yet somehow the spirit of classic Caesar salad
shines through in all of its tart, creamy, salty glory, proving that
recipes don't have to be faithful in order to be evocative.

To prepare the tempeh, put the cubes in a shallow glass bowl or
container, preferably one large enough to fit all of the tempeh in a
single layer. In a small bowl or measuring cup, combine the lemon
juice, tamari, mustard, agave nectar, pepper, and oil and whisk
until evenly combined. Pour the mixture over the tempeh and stir
gently to evenly coat the tempeh. Cover and refrigerate for at least
2 hours and up to 12 hours.

Preheat the oven to 350°F (175°C) and line two rimmed baking
sheets with parchment paper. Spread the tempeh cubes on one
lined baking sheet and dust with a grinding of pepper.

To prepare the croutons, spread the bread cubes on the other
lined baking sheet and drizzle with the oil. Toss the bread cubes
until evenly coated, then spread them in an even layer. Sprinkle
with the garlic powder and season with salt.

Place both baking sheets in the oven. Bake the bread cubes for
10 to 15 minutes, until golden and crispy. Bake the tempeh
for 15 to 20 minutes, until the edges are golden brown.

To make the dressing, put all the ingredients in a blender
(preferably a high-speed blender) and process until smooth.

To assemble the salad, put the kale, lettuce, and sun-dried
tomatoes in a large bowl. Add half of the dressing and toss gently
until evenly coated. Add the tempeh and croutons, pour in the
remaining dressing, and toss again. Serve right away.

BELUGA LENTILS AND TOMATOES
WITH TEMPEH BACON AND
TURMERIC MUSTARD VINAIGRETTE

This colorful salad is loosely inspired by the idea of a BLT—but with a couple of key twists. The "bacon" is my homemade Tempeh Bacon, which I use in breakfast burritos, as an accompaniment to morning scrambles, or on sandwiches. And in lieu of mayonnaise, the dressing is a tangy, vibrant mustard vinaigrette enhanced with turmeric, which turns the entire salad a beautiful shade of gold.

———————————————————

Cook the lentils as directed on page 15. Drain, rinse under cold running water, then let drain completely.

Meanwhile, prepare the bacon. In a small bowl, whisk together the tamari, vinegar, maple syrup, paprika, and cumin. Place the tempeh strips in a shallow glass bowl or container large enough to fit all of the tempeh in a single layer and pour the marinade over them. Flip the tempeh strips over to coat them evenly. Heat 1 teaspoon of the oil in a small skillet over medium heat. When the oil is shimmering, remove the tempeh strips from the marinade and put them in the skillet (reserve the marinade). Cook for 2 to 3 minutes on each side, until golden brown and slightly crispy, adding a bit more oil as needed to prevent sticking. Return the cooked tempeh to the baking pan with the marinade and let the strips sit while you finish the salad.

To make the dressing, combine all the ingredients in a small bowl or measuring cup and whisk until evenly blended.

Bring a medium pot of water to a boil. Add the corn and blanch for about 2 minutes, until tender. Drain immediately.

Put the kale in a large bowl and add three-quarters of the dressing. Using your hands, massage the dressing into the kale until it's softened. Add the corn, tomato, onion, and lentils. Toss again, then taste and add more dressing by the tablespoon as desired. To serve, crumble the bacon into the salad and toss it again, or divide the salad among serving plates and top each plate with whole strips of the bacon.

MAKES 4 SERVINGS OF SALAD, AND ABOUT ⅔ CUP (160 ML) OF DRESSING

⅔ cup (135 g) dried beluga or French green lentils

TEMPEH BACON

1½ tablespoons tamari

1 tablespoon apple cider vinegar

1 tablespoon maple syrup

¼ teaspoon smoked paprika

⅛ teaspoon ground cumin

8 ounces (225 g) tempeh, sliced into strips ¼ inch (6 mm) thick

1 to 2 teaspoons neutral vegetable oil

DRESSING

3 tablespoons olive oil

3 tablespoons tahini

3 tablespoons apple cider vinegar

1 tablespoon Dijon mustard

1 tablespoon agave nectar or maple syrup

1 teaspoon ground turmeric

¼ teaspoon salt

⅛ teaspoon freshly ground black pepper

1½ cups (235 g) fresh or frozen corn kernels

1 bunch curly kale, stemmed and chopped

1 large tomato, chopped, or 1½ cups (225 g) cherry tomatoes, halved or quartered

½ small red onion, diced

BROWN RICE TABBOULEH SALAD

Traditional tabbouleh is made with bulgur wheat, and alternative versions are usually made with another small grain, such as quinoa. I like using brown rice to give a heartier and more toothsome quality to this beloved dish. The finished recipe feels like a cross between tabbouleh and Greek rice, or *spanakorizo*, which is also made with freshly chopped herbs, a touch of garlic, and plenty of lemon juice. I add chickpeas for protein, but feel free to substitute lentils, navy beans, or another legume.

MAKES 3 TO 4 SERVINGS

1 cup (185 g) medium- or long-grain brown rice

1½ cups (60 g) firmly packed fresh parsley

½ cup (15 g) firmly packed fresh mint leaves

2 scallions, green and pale green parts, coarsely chopped

1 small clove garlic, coarsely chopped

2 to 3 tablespoons olive oil

2 tablespoons freshly squeezed lemon juice

¾ teaspoon salt

¼ teaspoon freshly ground black pepper

2 tomatoes, diced

1 cucumber, peeled and diced

1½ cups (250 g) cooked chickpeas, or 1 (15-oz, or 425-g) can, drained and rinsed

Cook the rice as directed on page 12. When the rice is ready, remove it from the heat, fluff it gently with a fork, and set the rice aside to cool for at least 20 minutes while you prepare the rest of the salad.

Combine the parsley, mint, scallions, and garlic in a food processor and pulse or process until finely chopped and uniform; alternatively, mince the parsley, mint, scallions, and garlic by hand.

In a small bowl or measuring cup, whisk together 2 tablespoons of the oil and the lemon juice, salt, and pepper.

In a large bowl, combine the tomatoes, cucumber, chickpeas, rice, and chopped herbs. Pour in the dressing and stir until thoroughly combined. Taste and add more of the oil if you like. Taste again and adjust the seasonings if desired. Serve chilled or at room temperature.

SOUPS

The soups I love best are thick and hearty—the kind of soups that make for a perfectly satisfying dinner when served with a hunk of bread. I might make gazpacho or some other light, summery soup as an appetizer when friends come over, but those are rarely the soups I make for myself.

In this chapter you'll find a collection of my favorite soups, each a meal in itself, packed with legumes and vegetables—and therefore with protein, fiber, and plenty of other nutrients. You'll find some of my longtime favorites, including an easy white bean-laden ribollita (page 116), a richly spiced African-inspired stew with peanuts and chickpeas (page 115), and, perhaps my favorite, a creamy split pea and corn chowder (page 120).

Many of these soups feature leafy greens, such as kale or collard greens. I'm always on the lookout for opportunities to pack more greens into my diet, and soups are a great vehicle for them. Even the soups that don't call for greens can be modified to include them. Just stir chopped leafy greens into a soup 5 to 10 minutes before the end of the cooking time. The greens will wilt into the soup. Alternatively, you could stir in chopped zucchini, broccoli, asparagus, or any vegetable you love. And while all these soups feature at least one source of protein, you can make them even heartier by topping them with Tempeh Bacon (see page 97), Roasted Chickpeas (see page 104), or your favorite vegan meat.

Many soups can be pulled together using basic pantry ingredients, and I always keep my cupboards stocked accordingly with dried legumes, whole grains, canned tomatoes, and dried herbs. Homemade vegetable stock is lovely, but vegan bouillon cubes and store-bought vegetable stock are just fine—and they're what I usually use at home.

Most of these soups make six servings. If you're cooking for a crowd, great; if not, that isn't a problem. Many of these soups keep well in the refrigerator for several days, and any leftovers can be frozen for longer storage. That way, you'll have nutritious meals on hand for those busy times when it's difficult to cook.

SMOKY RED LENTIL STEW
WITH CHARD

One of the advantages of using red lentils in soup is that they cook amazingly fast. This soup has a deep, smoky flavor, as if it's been simmered for hours, but it's comes together in about 30 minutes.

MAKES 6 TO 8 SERVINGS

1 tablespoon olive oil

1 white or yellow onion, chopped

2 carrots, peeled and chopped

2 stalks celery, chopped

3 cloves garlic, minced

1 large sweet potato, peeled and cut into ¾-inch (2-cm) cubes

1 teaspoon smoked paprika

½ teaspoon dried thyme

½ teaspoon dried rosemary

¾ teaspoon salt

¼ teaspoon freshly ground black pepper

1½ cups (300 g) dried red lentils

4 cups (950 ml) low-sodium vegetable broth

1½ cups (355 ml) water

2 tablespoons freshly squeezed lemon juice

1 small bunch Swiss chard or other greens, stemmed and chopped

Heat the oil in a large pot over medium heat. Add the onion, carrots, and celery and cook, stirring occasionally, for 5 to 7 minutes, until the onion is tender and translucent. Add the garlic and cook, stirring constantly, for 1 to 2 minutes, until the garlic is fragrant.

Stir in the sweet potato, paprika, thyme, rosemary, salt, and pepper, then stir in the lentils, broth, and water. Bring to a boil over high heat, then lower the heat, cover, and simmer for about 20 minutes, until the sweet potato is tender and lentils seem to have melted into the soup.

Stir in the lemon juice and chard. Cover and simmer for 3 to 5 minutes, until the chard has wilted completely. Taste and adjust the seasonings if desired. Serve piping hot.

CHEESY CREAM OF BROCCOLI
WITH SMOKY ROASTED CHICKPEAS

One of my first and most memorable kitchen disasters—and I mean a truly failed recipe, not just something that needed tweaking—was a vegan broccoli soup that I totally overwhelmed with lemon. I've since learned to be judicious in adding acid to my soups, and I love the balance of flavors here. The soup is equal parts garlicky, savory, and cheesy, with a hint of lemon. To add some texture, I top it with sweet and smoky roasted chickpeas. The chickpeas are great in salads or served over savory oats, so you may want to make a double batch!

———————————————

To roast the chickpeas, preheat the oven to 400°F (200°C) and line a rimmed baking sheet with parchment paper. In a medium bowl, toss the chickpeas with the oil until evenly coated. Sprinkle with the paprika, chili powder, cayenne, and salt and toss again. Transfer to the lined baking sheet and bake for 30 to 40 minutes, until crispy, stirring a few times as they bake.

Meanwhile, make the soup. Heat the oil in a large pot over medium heat. Add the onion and celery and cook, stirring occasionally, for 5 to 7 minutes, until the onion is tender and translucent. Add the garlic and cook, stirring constantly, for 2 minutes.

Stir in the broccoli, potatoes, salt, oregano, bay leaf, and paprika, then pour in the broth. Bring to a boil over high heat. Lower the heat, cover, and simmer for 20 minutes, until the potatoes are fork-tender. Remove the bay leaf.

Use an immersion blender to puree the soup, or puree it in batches in a standard blender and return it to the pot. Stir in the lemon juice, nondairy milk, and nutritional yeast. If the soup is thicker than you'd like, stir in more broth as needed to achieve the desired consistency. Season with black pepper to taste, and adjust lemon and salt as needed.

Serve, topped with the chickpeas.

MAKES 4 TO 6 SERVINGS

ROASTED CHICKPEAS

1½ cups (250 g) cooked chickpeas, or 1 (15-oz, or 425-g) can, drained and rinsed

2 teaspoons neutral vegetable oil

1 teaspoon smoked paprika

½ teaspoon chili powder

Pinch of cayenne pepper

½ teaspoon salt

SOUP

1 tablespoon neutral vegetable oil

1 white or yellow onion, chopped

2 stalks celery, diced

6 cloves garlic, minced

1½ pounds (680 g) broccoli, coarsely chopped

2 large or 3 small Yukon gold potatoes, peeled and coarsely chopped

1 teaspoon salt

1 teaspoon dried oregano

1 bay leaf

¾ teaspoon smoked paprika

5 cups (1.2 L) low-sodium vegetable broth, plus more if needed

2 teaspoons freshly squeezed lemon juice

1 cup (240 ml) unsweetened nondairy milk

¼ cup (20 g) nutritional yeast

Freshly ground black pepper

CURRIED TOMATO STEW
WITH CHICKPEA DUMPLINGS

The idea for this stew with chickpea dumplings was inspired by a wonderful recipe on Shelly Westerhausen's *Vegetarian Ventures* food blog. I've incorporated red lentils, which are an easy and sneaky protein source for saucy dishes. I've always loved the idea of savory dumplings, but I never had success with them until I tried this recipe, which calls for chickpea flour, rather than wheat flour. The dumplings are tender and savory, not to mention rich in protein.

MAKES 4 SERVINGS

STEW BASE

1 tablespoon olive oil

1 small white or yellow onion, diced

4 cloves garlic, minced

½ teaspoon ground turmeric

1 teaspoon sweet paprika

2 teaspoons curry powder

1 (28-oz, or 794-g) can crushed tomatoes

⅔ cup (135 g) dried red lentils

1¾ cups (415 ml) low-sodium vegetable broth

½ teaspoon salt

¼ teaspoon red pepper flakes

4 cups firmly packed baby spinach (120 g) or chopped kale (260 g)

DUMPLINGS

1½ cups (180 g) chickpea flour

½ teaspoon salt

½ teaspoon baking powder

½ teaspoon ground cumin

2 tablespoons minced fresh parsley

1 scallion, green parts only, finely chopped

½ cup (120 ml) water, plus more if needed

Scallions, green parts only, chopped, for garnish

To make the stew base, heat the oil in a large pot over medium heat. Add the onion and cook, stirring occasionally, for 5 to 7 minutes, until the onion is tender and translucent. Add the garlic and cook, stirring constantly, for 2 minutes.

Stir in the turmeric, paprika, curry powder, tomatoes, lentils, and broth. Bring to a boil, then lower the heat, cover, and simmer for 15 minutes. Stir in the salt and red pepper flakes, then add the spinach without stirring it in. Cover the pan and let the spinach steam for 5 minutes.

Meanwhile, make the dumplings. In a medium bowl, combine the flour, salt, baking powder, cumin, parsley, and scallion. Add the water and use a wooden spoon to stir until all the ingredients come together. The dough should be fairly stiff (similar to biscuit dough), but if it's too stiff or dry to mix well, add more water by the tablespoonful until the dough holds together.

Give the stew a good stir, mixing in all of the spinach. Using about 2 tablespoons dough per dumpling, drop the dumpling dough on top of stew (a cookie scoop can be useful here); you should end up with about 12 dumplings. Cover the pot and let the dumplings steam for about 8 minutes, until firm. Serve right away, garnished with the scallions.

SPICY CABBAGE SOUP
WITH RICE AND CHICKPEAS

This soup is my grown-up answer to the chicken soup that kept me company through childhood illnesses, rainy days, and long winters. It's as comforting as my mom's (and like hers, it's heavy on the lemon), but I've made it my own by replacing chicken with chickpeas, doubling the amount of cabbage, and adding the kick of turmeric and paprika. It's a wonderful soup to make when you're fighting off a cold or simply in need of nourishment and care. If you really want to channel childhood nostalgia, try using noodles or small, shaped pasta in place of the rice.

_____

MAKES 6 TO 8 SERVINGS

1 tablespoon olive oil

1 white or yellow onion, chopped

3 carrots, peeled and diced

2 stalks celery, diced

3 cloves garlic, minced

6½ cups (450 g) shredded green cabbage

1 cup (185 g) medium- or long-grain brown rice

1 teaspoon sweet paprika

1 teaspoon ground turmeric

1 teaspoon salt

8 cups (1.9 L) low-sodium vegetable broth

2 cups (475 ml) water

3 cups (500 g) cooked chickpeas, or 2 (15-oz, or 425-g) cans, drained and rinsed

2 tablespoons freshly squeezed lemon juice

Freshly ground black pepper

Pinch of red pepper flakes (optional)

Parsley, chopped (optional)

Heat the oil in a large pot over medium heat. Add the onion, carrots, and celery and cook, stirring occasionally, for 5 to 7 minutes, until the onion is translucent and tender. Add the garlic and cook, stirring constantly, for 2 minutes.

Stir in the cabbage, rice, paprika, turmeric, and salt, then pour in the broth and water. Bring to a boil over high heat. Lower the heat, cover, and simmer for about 45 minutes, until the rice is tender.

Stir in the chickpeas and lemon juice and cook just until the chickpeas are heated through. Season to taste with black pepper. Serve piping hot, with a garnish of crushed red pepper flakes and fresh parsley.

MOROCCAN TAGINE
WITH TEMPEH AND CHICKPEAS

This stew is reminiscent of ratatouille, but it's easier to make, and heartier too. It features two powerhouse plant protein sources—chickpeas and tempeh—along with dried fruit, which provides a subtle contrast to the earthiness of the tempeh and tartness of the tomatoes. Some people consider salting eggplant prior to cooking to be unnecessary, but I think it makes a big difference, especially if the eggplant isn't quite ripe.

MAKES 4 SERVINGS

1 small eggplant, cubed

Coarse salt

1 tablespoon plus 2 teaspoons olive oil

8 ounces (225 g) tempeh, cut into 32 cubes

Salt and freshly ground black pepper

1 red onion, coarsely chopped

6 cloves garlic, minced

2 tablespoons finely grated or minced fresh ginger

1 medium zucchini, cubed

2 tomatoes, chopped, or 1 (14.5-oz, or 411-g) can diced tomatoes, drained

1½ cups (250 g) cooked chickpeas, or 1 (15-oz, or 425-g) can, drained and rinsed

2 teaspoons ground cumin

1 teaspoon ground coriander

¼ teaspoon ground cinnamon

¼ teaspoon ground allspice

Generous pinch of red pepper flakes

Heaping ⅓ cup (about 60 g) golden raisins, currants, or finely chopped dried apricots or prunes

2 cups (475 ml) water

2 to 3 teaspoons red wine vinegar

OPTIONAL ACCOMPANIMENTS
Cooked quinoa, bulgur wheat, or other whole grain; chopped fresh parsley or cilantro; lemon wedges

Put the eggplant in a large colander, sprinkle generously with coarse salt, and toss to coat. Let sit for 25 to 30 minutes, then rinse under cold running water. Dry with paper towels or a clean kitchen towel, pressing to extract as much moisture as possible.

Meanwhile, heat 2 teaspoons of the oil over medium-high heat in a large pot. Add the tempeh and sprinkle with a pinch each of salt and pepper. Cook, flipping the tempeh frequently, for 7 to 8 minutes, until browned on all sides. Transfer to a plate or small bowl.

Add the remaining 1 tablespoon oil to the same pot over medium heat. Add the onion and cook, stirring occasionally, for 5 to 7 minutes, until tender and translucent. Add the garlic and ginger and cook, stirring constantly, for 2 minutes.

Stir in the zucchini, tomatoes, chickpeas, cumin, coriander, cinnamon, allspice, red pepper flakes, and ¾ teaspoon salt, then stir in the dried fruit and water. Bring to a simmer, then lower the heat, cover, and simmer for 20 minutes, stirring every 5 minutes or so. Remove the lid and cook, stirring occasionally, for 5 to 8 minutes, until the stew has thickened up and the eggplant is very tender.

Stir in the tempeh and red wine vinegar. Taste the stew and adjust the seasonings if desired. Serve the stew with a cooked whole grain, parsley or cilantro, and lemon wedges.

WHITE BEAN SOUP
WITH LEEKS AND ROASTED CAULIFLOWER

Roasting the cauliflower before adding it to this creamy soup results in surprising depth of flavor. Just pop the cauliflower in the oven before you begin chopping the remaining ingredients, and by the time the broth is ready, the cauliflower should be, too. I love the richness of this soup and think it's perfect for cold winter nights. For a comforting and well-rounded meal, pair it with a fresh green salad and toast.

MAKES 6 SERVINGS

1 medium cauliflower, trimmed and cut into bite-size pieces

3 tablespoons olive oil

Coarse salt

3 leeks, white parts only, chopped

2 stalks celery, diced

2 shallots, thinly sliced

3 cloves garlic, minced

3 cups (540 g) cooked navy, Great Northern, or cannellini beans, or 2 (15-oz, or 425-g) cans, drained and rinsed

6 cups (1.4 L) low-sodium vegetable broth

2 tablespoons chopped fresh rosemary leaves, or 2 teaspoons dried rosemary

1 tablespoon fresh thyme leaves, or 1½ teaspoons dried thyme

1 tablespoon chopped fresh sage, or 1 teaspoon dried sage

2 bay leaves

1 teaspoon salt

¼ teaspoon freshly ground black pepper

2 tablespoons freshly squeezed lemon juice

¼ cup (60 ml) Cheesy Hemp Seed Topping (see page 89) or vegan parmesan, plus more for topping

Preheat the oven to 400°F (200°C) and line a rimmed baking sheet with parchment paper. In a large bowl, toss the cauliflower with 2 tablespoons of the oil until evenly coated. Spread the cauliflower on the lined baking sheet and sprinkle with coarse salt. Bake for 35 to 40 minutes, until browned, stirring once halfway through baking.

Meanwhile, heat the remaining 1 tablespoon oil in a large pot over medium heat. Add the leeks, celery, and shallots and cook, stirring frequently, for 5 to 7 minutes, until the leeks are translucent and the celery is tender. Add the garlic and cook, stirring constantly, for 1 minute.

Stir in the beans, broth, rosemary, thyme, sage, bay leaves, salt, and pepper. Bring to a boil over high heat, then lower the heat, cover, and simmer for 15 to 20 minutes while the cauliflower finishes roasting so that the beans can absorb flavor.

Remove the bay leaves and stir in the cauliflower. Use an immersion blender to puree the soup, or puree it in batches in a standard blender and return it to the pot. Stir in the lemon juice and hemp seed topping. If the soup is thicker than you'd like, stir in a bit of water to achieve the desired consistency. Taste and adjust the seasonings if desired. Serve piping hot, with as much extra hemp seed topping as you like!

WEST AFRICAN PEANUT STEW
WITH SWEET POTATOES AND CHICKPEAS

This is a variation on a rich, fragrant stew that I've been making for years. Peanuts, tomatoes, and greens are staple ingredients in central and west African cooking, and they pair wonderfully with ginger, garlic, and chiles—the latter in the form of chili powder and harissa in this recipe. Sweet potatoes and chickpeas add body to the stew, and if you serve it over warm cooked millet (a staple grain in many parts of Africa) or another grain, it makes for an extremely hearty meal.

MAKES 6 SERVINGS

1 tablespoon olive oil

1 small white or yellow onion, chopped

4 cloves garlic, minced

2 tablespoons finely grated or minced fresh ginger, or 2 teaspoons ground ginger

1 teaspoon ground coriander

½ teaspoon chili powder

1 tablespoon harissa paste, or additional 1 teaspoon chili powder

¾ teaspoon salt

2 medium sweet potatoes, peeled and diced

6 cups (1.4 L) low-sodium vegetable broth

1 (14.5-oz, or 411-g) can diced tomatoes, preferably fire-roasted

¼ cup (65 g) tomato paste

⅓ cup (85 g) smooth peanut butter or sunflower seed butter

3 cups (500 g) cooked chickpeas, or 2 (15-oz, or 425-g) cans, drained and rinsed

1 small bunch collard greens, stemmed and cut into thin strips

4 cups cooked millet, brown rice, or quinoa (optional)

Chopped roasted peanuts, for topping

Chopped scallions, green parts only, for topping

Heat the oil in a large pot over medium heat. Add the onion and cook, stirring occasionally, for 5 minutes, until the onion is tender and translucent. Add the garlic and ginger and cook, stirring constantly, for 1 minute, adding about a tablespoonful of water if the ginger starts to stick.

Stir in the coriander, chili powder, harissa, salt, and sweet potatoes, then stir in the broth and tomatoes. Bring to a boil over high heat, then lower the heat, cover, and simmer for 20 minutes.

Put the tomato paste and peanut butter in a medium bowl and add about 1½ cups (360 ml) hot liquid from the soup. Whisk to create a slurry, then add the slurry to the soup and stir well. For a smoother consistency, use an immersion blender to partially puree the soup, or puree a portion of it in a standard blender and return it to the pot.

Stir in the chickpeas and greens. Cover and simmer for 5 to 10 minutes, until the greens are wilted. Taste and adjust the seasonings if desired. Serve over millet, topped with peanuts and scallions.

WHITE BEAN RIBOLLITA

Ribollita is everything I want to eat on a cold night: fragrant, garlicky broth with plenty of vegetables, and crusty, rustic bread to soak it up. It's a great vehicle for using up vegetable odds and ends and day-old bread. And although the recipe calls for white beans, kidney beans or chickpeas would be a fine alternative. This soup is plenty satisfying, but for an even more filling meal, try serving it with my tempeh sausage crumbles (or your favorite vegan sausage).

MAKES 6 TO 8 SERVINGS

2 tablespoons olive oil, plus more for drizzling (optional)

1 large white or yellow onion, diced

3 carrots, peeled and diced

3 stalks celery, diced

8 ounces (225 g) green cabbage, coarsely chopped

Salt

5 cloves garlic, minced or finely grated

¼ teaspoon freshly ground black pepper

5 cups (1.2 L) low-sodium vegetable broth, plus more if desired

1 (28-oz, or 794-g) can crushed or diced tomatoes

3 cups (540 g) cooked cannellini, Great Northern, or navy beans, or 2 (15-oz, or 425-g) cans, drained and rinsed

1 bunch Lacinato kale, stemmed and cut into thin strips

¼ cup (20 g) nutritional yeast, Cheesy Hemp Seed Topping (see page 89), or store-bought vegan parmesan, plus more for topping

1¾ cups Savory Tempeh Sausage Crumbles (optional; page 185) or store-bought vegan sausage, cooked if necessary, then sliced or crumbled

4 slices whole grain bread, toasted

Heat the oil in a large pot over medium heat. Add the onion, carrots, celery, cabbage, and a pinch of salt and cook, stirring occasionally, for 7 to 8 minutes, until the onion and cabbage are tender. Add the garlic and cook, stirring constantly, for 1 minute.

Stir in 1 teaspoon salt and the pepper, broth, tomatoes, and beans. Bring to a boil over high heat, then lower the heat, cover, and simmer for 15 minutes.

Add the kale, cover, and simmer for 3 to 5 minutes, until the kale has wilted. Stir in the nutritional yeast and sausage crumbles. If the soup is thicker than you'd like, stir in more broth as needed to achieve the desired consistency. Taste and adjust the seasonings if desired.

For each serving, place a slice of the toasted bread in a shallow bowl. Ladle the soup over the bread. Serve right away, topped with nutritional yeast and a drizzle of oil.

CURRIED JAMAICAN STEW
WITH KIDNEY BEANS

This recipe is simple enough to make, but don't be fooled: it's incredibly rich and flavorful. The stew features traditional Jamaican seasonings, including red pepper flakes, allspice, and cloves, as well as a generous swirl of coconut milk. Many Jamaican recipes call for Indian curry powder, rather than Thai curry paste, but I enjoy how the garlic and heat of the paste give this soup a kick.

MAKES 6 SERVINGS

1 tablespoon coconut oil

1 white or yellow onion, diced

1 green bell pepper, diced

1 jalapeño chile, finely diced

2 tomatoes, chopped, or 1 (14.5-oz, 411-g) can diced tomatoes

1 tablespoon red curry paste

1 teaspoon salt

1 teaspoon ground allspice

¾ teaspoon red pepper flakes

½ teaspoon ground cumin

½ teaspoon ground cinnamon

¼ teaspoon ground cloves

3 cups (540 g) cooked kidney beans, or 2 (15-oz, or 425-g) cans, drained and rinsed

4 medium sweet potatoes, peeled and cut into ½-inch (1.3-cm) cubes

3 cups (710 ml) low-sodium vegetable broth or water, plus more if desired

1 small or ½ medium bunch collard greens or other greens, stemmed and cut into thin strips

1 cup (240 ml) full-fat coconut milk

¼ cup (25 g) chopped scallions, green and white parts, plus more for topping

Heat the oil in a large pot over medium heat. Add the onion, bell pepper, and jalapeño and cook, stirring occasionally, for 5 to 7 minutes, until the onion is tender and translucent. Add the tomatoes and red curry paste and cook, stirring frequently, for about 5 minutes, until the tomatoes have released their juices and cooked down a bit.

Stir in the salt, allspice, red pepper flakes, cumin, cinnamon, cloves, beans, and sweet potatoes, then pour in the broth. Bring to a boil over medium-high heat, then lower the heat and simmer, stirring occasionally, for 20 minutes.

Use an immersion blender to partially puree the soup so that about half of the sweet potato cubes and kidney beans are still visible and whole, or puree about half of the soup in a standard blender and return it to the pot. Add the collard greens and simmer for 5 to 10 minutes, until the greens have wilted. Stir in the coconut milk and scallions. If the soup is thicker than you'd like, stir in more broth to achieve the desired consistency. Taste and adjust seasonings if desired. Serve with extra chopped scallions.

YELLOW SPLIT PEA CHOWDER
WITH SWEET CORN

Think of this soup as a marriage of split pea soup and traditional corn chowder. The split peas give the soup body and nutrition, along with a gorgeous golden color. Meanwhile, adding Cashew Cream to the finished soup gives it a rich, creamy, luxurious texture. I make this soup in late August or early September, when corn is at its sweetest, and I almost always serve it with crumbled Tempeh Bacon and chives on top.

MAKES 6 SERVINGS

1 tablespoon olive oil

1 white or yellow onion, chopped

2 stalks celery, diced

3 cloves garlic, minced

6 cups (1.4 L) low-sodium vegetable broth

1 cup (200 g) yellow split peas, soaked for 1 hour and drained

1 medium Yukon gold or russet potato, peeled and chopped

Kernels from 4 ears sweet white or yellow corn (about 2½ cups, or 360 g)

¾ teaspoon smoked paprika

1 teaspoon salt

¾ cup (180 ml) Cashew Cream (see page 182)

1 small bunch collard greens, stemmed and chopped

OPTIONAL TOPPINGS

Chopped fresh chives or scallions, Tempeh Bacon (see page 97), chopped red bell pepper

Heat the oil in a large pot over medium heat. Add the onion and celery and cook, stirring occasionally, for 5 to 7 minutes, until the onion is tender and translucent. Add the garlic and cook, stirring constantly, for 1 minute.

Stir in the broth, split peas, potato, corn, paprika, and salt and bring to a boil over high heat. Lower the heat, cover, and simmer, stirring occasionally, for about 45 minutes, until the split peas are completely tender.

Use an immersion blender to partially puree the soup, or puree about half of it in a standard blender and return it to the pot. Stir in the Cashew Cream and collard greens and cook, stirring occasionally, until the greens are tender and wilted, 5 to 10 minutes. Taste and adjust the seasonings if desired. Serve piping hot, with any desired toppings.

MUSHROOM MISO BARLEY SOUP

I love the combination of mushrooms and barley, and also the combination of mushrooms and miso. This hearty, comforting soup is a tribute to both pairings. The flavors—garlic, thyme, onion, and lemon—are reminiscent of traditional mushroom barley soup, but the miso offers up another layer of richness and umami.

MAKES 6 TO 8 SERVINGS

1 tablespoon olive oil

1 white or yellow onion, diced

2 carrots, peeled and diced

2 stalks celery, diced

1 pound (450 g) mushrooms, any variety, sliced

3 cloves garlic, minced

Coarse salt

1 cup (200 g) pearl barley

1 tablespoon fresh thyme leaves, or 1 teaspoon dried thyme

8 cups (1.9 L) low-sodium vegetable broth

3 tablespoons white miso

1 small bunch Lacinato or curly kale, stemmed and cut into thin strips

8 ounces (225 g) smoked or baked tofu, diced; or 1½ cups (250 g) cooked chickpeas, or 1 (15-oz, or 425-g) can, drained and rinsed (optional)

Freshly ground black pepper

Freshly squeezed lemon juice

Heat the oil in a large pot over medium heat. Add the onion, carrots, and celery and cook, stirring occasionally, for 5 to 7 minutes, until the onion is tender and translucent. Add the mushrooms, garlic, and a generous pinch of salt. Cook, stirring frequently, for 5 to 7 minutes, until the mushrooms have released their juices and are tender.

Stir in the barley, thyme, and broth. Bring to a boil over high heat, then lower the heat and simmer, stirring occasionally, for 25 to 30 minutes, until the barley is plump and tender.

Put the miso into a small bowl and add about ¼ cup (60 ml) of the hot liquid from the soup. Whisk to create a slurry, then add the slurry to the soup and stir well. Stir in the kale, cover, and simmer for 3 to 5 minutes, until the kale has wilted. Stir in the tofu or another protein and heat through. Season with pepper and lemon juice to taste. Serve piping hot.

TORTILLA SOUP
WITH ROASTED CORN
AND BLACK BEAN SALSA

SALSA

3 cups (465 g) fresh or frozen yellow corn kernels

1 large red onion, chopped

2 poblano chiles, chopped

2 tablespoons neutral vegetable oil

1 teaspoon ground cumin

1 teaspoon chili powder

Pinch of cayenne pepper

Coarse salt

1½ cups (270 g) cooked black beans, or 1 (15-oz, or 425-g) can, drained and rinsed

2 tablespoons freshly squeezed lime juice

SOUP

1 tablespoon olive oil

1 Vidalia or yellow onion, chopped

2 carrots, peeled and chopped

4 cloves garlic, finely minced

1 (28-oz, or 794-g) can diced tomatoes, preferably fire-roasted

1 to 2 tablespoons chopped chipotles in adobo with their sauce

1 teaspoon ground cumin

½ teaspoon ground coriander

½ teaspoon salt

4 cups (950 ml) low-sodium vegetable broth

6 (6-in, or 15-cm) corn tortillas, torn into pieces

OPTIONAL ACCOMPANIMENTS

Tortilla chips, cooked brown or white rice, shredded vegan chicken strips or Savory Tempeh Sausage Crumbles (see page 185), shredded vegan cheese

This soup can be made almost entirely from pantry ingredients, and if you keep black beans and frozen corn on hand, the salsa is equally convenient. When I serve this soup for lunch, I like to pair it with the salsa and some crunchy corn chips; to turn it into a more filling evening meal, I often stir in cooked long-grain rice or top it with shredded vegan chicken strips. If you begin to prepare the soup while the vegetables for the salsa are roasting, both components should be ready at about the same time.

———————————————

To make the salsa, preheat the oven to 400°F (200°C) and line a rimmed baking sheet with parchment paper. In a large bowl, combine the corn, onion, and poblanos. Drizzle with the oil and toss until evenly coated. Sprinkle with the cumin, chili powder, and cayenne and toss again. Transfer to the lined baking sheet, spreading the mixture evenly, then sprinkle generously with coarse salt. Bake for 20 minutes, until the onion and corn are slightly browned, stirring once or twice during the baking time.

Transfer the roasted vegetables to a bowl. Add the black beans and lime juice and stir gently to combine. Taste and adjust the seasonings if desired.

To make the soup, heat the oil in a large pot over medium heat. Add the onion and carrots and cook, stirring occasionally, for 5 to 7 minutes, until the onion is tender and translucent. Add the garlic and cook, stirring constantly, for 1 minute.

Stir in the tomatoes, chipotles in adobo, cumin, coriander, and salt, then stir in the broth. Bring to a boil over medium-high heat, then lower the heat to maintain a simmer. Add the tortillas, cover, and cook for 10 minutes.

Use an immersion blender to puree the soup, or puree it in batches in a standard blender and return it to the pot. Taste and adjust the seasonings if desired. Serve topped with the salsa and any other desired accompaniments.

MULLIGATAWNY

Mulligatawny is a fusion dish, a cultural hybrid that's thought to have emerged during the British colonization of India. It features some of the same spices that appear in most curries, along with the surprising addition of apples and celery, plus a handful of basmati rice, cooked in the soup to help thicken it. Whereas the soup is usually made with chicken, I make mine with red or yellow lentils, and I always top it with a big handful of fresh herbs.

MAKES 6 SERVINGS

1 tablespoon olive oil

1 large white or yellow onion, chopped

2 large carrots, peeled and chopped

2 stalks celery, chopped

3 cloves garlic, minced

2 teaspoons finely grated or minced fresh ginger

1 tablespoon curry powder

1 teaspoon ground turmeric

½ teaspoon ground coriander

¾ teaspoon salt

2 small or medium apples, peeled and chopped

1 cup (200 g) dried red or yellow lentils

⅓ cup (60 g) white basmati rice

1 (14.5-oz, or 411-g) can diced tomatoes

6 cups (1.4 L) low-sodium vegetable broth

¼ cup (60 ml) full-fat coconut milk or Cashew Cream (see page 182)

Freshly squeezed lime juice

Freshly ground black pepper

Shredded vegan chicken strips (optional)

OPTIONAL TOPPINGS

Chopped fresh cilantro, chopped scallions, chopped fresh chives

Heat the oil in a large pot over medium heat. Add the onion, carrots, and celery and cook, stirring frequently, for 5 to 7 minutes, until the onion is translucent and the carrots are just tender. Add the garlic and ginger and cook, stirring constantly, for 2 minutes, adding about a tablespoonful of water if the ginger starts to stick.

Stir in the curry powder, turmeric, coriander, salt, apples, lentils, rice, and tomatoes, then stir in the broth. Bring to a boil over high heat, then lower the heat, cover, and simmer, stirring occasionally, for 25 minutes, until the lentils are tender but not mushy.

Leave the soup chunky if you like; alternatively, use an immersion blender to partially puree the soup, or puree a portion of it in a standard blender and return it to the pot. Stir in the coconut milk and a squeeze of lime juice and season with pepper. Stir in some shredded vegan chicken strips. Taste and adjust the seasonings if desired. Serve piping hot, with chopped fresh herbs.

LEMONY LENTIL SOUP
WITH MUSHROOMS AND KALE

I usually add more than the suggested amount of lemon juice to this highly nutritious soup, but that's because I'm a lemon fiend. No matter how much lemon juice you add, this soup is packed with plant protein and wholesome ingredients and will do your body good.

MAKES 6 SERVINGS

1½ tablespoons olive oil

1 large white or yellow onion, chopped

4 carrots, peeled and diced

2 stalks celery, diced

3 cloves garlic, minced

8 ounces (225 g) white mushrooms, sliced

Salt

1½ teaspoons dried thyme

½ teaspoon dried rosemary

¼ teaspoon freshly ground black pepper

1½ cups (300 g) dried green, brown, or French green lentils

4 cups (950 ml) low-sodium vegetable broth

2 cups (475 ml) water

1 small bunch kale, stemmed and chopped

3 tablespoons freshly squeezed lemon juice

Heat the oil in a large pot over medium heat. Add the onion, carrots, and celery and cook, stirring occasionally, for 8 minutes, until the vegetables are tender. Stir in the garlic, mushrooms, and a generous pinch of salt. Cover and cook for 5 minutes, until the mushrooms are tender and have released their juices.

Stir in ½ teaspoon salt and the thyme, rosemary, pepper, and lentils, then pour in the broth and water. Bring to a boil over high heat, then lower the heat, cover partially, and simmer, stirring occasionally, for about 30 minutes, until the lentils are tender but not mushy. Stir in the kale, cover, and cook for 10 minutes. Stir in the lemon juice, then taste and adjust the seasonings if desired. Serve piping hot.

WHITE CHILI
WITH BUTTERNUT SQUASH

White chili, so-called because it's tomato-free and milder than traditional varieties, is generally made with a combination of white beans and green chiles. Mine is a departure because I add both chipotles in adobo and smoked paprika. I love how these smoky flavors contrast with the bright, piquant green chiles that are characteristic of the dish.

MAKES 6 SERVINGS

1 tablespoon olive oil

1 large white or yellow onion, chopped

3 cloves garlic, minced

3 cups (540 g) cooked navy, Great Northern, or cannellini beans, or 2 (15-oz, or 425-g) cans, drained and rinsed

1 small zucchini, cut into ¾-inch (2-cm) cubes

1½ pounds (680 g) butternut squash, peeled, seeded, and cut into ¾-inch (2-cm) cubes

2 (4-oz, or 113-g) cans mild green chiles with their liquid

2 tablespoons chopped chipotles in adobo with their sauce

1 teaspoon smoked paprika

1 teaspoon ground cumin

1 teaspoon chili powder

¾ teaspoon salt

⅔ cup (115 g) quinoa, rinsed

3 cups (710 ml) low-sodium vegetable broth

1 to 2 tablespoons freshly squeezed lime juice

Heat the oil in a large pot over medium heat. Add the onion and cook, stirring occasionally, for 5 to 7 minutes, until the onion is tender and translucent. Add the garlic and cook, stirring constantly, for 2 minutes.

Stir in the beans, zucchini, butternut squash, green chiles, chipotles in adobo, paprika, cumin, chili powder, salt, and quinoa, then pour in the broth. Bring to a boil over medium-high heat, then lower the heat, cover, and simmer for 20 minutes, until the butternut squash is fork-tender and the quinoa is fully cooked. Uncover and cook, stirring occasionally, for 5 minutes. Stir in the lime juice, then taste and adjust the seasonings if desired. Serve piping hot.

BOWLS

A few years ago, as I settled into the rhythms of working from home, I began a lunchtime tradition. After a weekend of batch cooking, I'd combine a few different grains, beans, and vegetables in a bowl, drizzle dressing over the top, and enjoy. There was no real cooking required, and it was an easy way to turn what was in my fridge into something greater than the sum of its parts.

I started taking photographs of the bowls and posting them on my Instagram account, and they quickly became some of my most popular posts. I was mystified by this at first—many of the other recipes I posted struck me as prettier—but over time I realized that people were responding to the same qualities that had captured me: simplicity, convenience, and variety, served up in a single vessel.

The recipes in this chapter are different from my everyday lunch bowls. They're more elaborate and feature intentional combinations of flavors and textures (in other words, they aren't just a vehicle for leftovers). But the idea behind them is the same: combining simple components in a creative way.

Some of the bowls, especially the heartier ones, like the Golden Rice Bowls with Tofu Paneer and Vegetables (page 140), are best served hot. Others can be served warm, at room temperature, or chilled. For the bowls that feature baby greens like arugula or spinach as a base, I recommend allowing your toppings to cool slightly before assembly so that the cooked components don't wilt the greens. You can mix all of the ingredients up with the sauce or dressing, or you can keep them separate and drizzle the dressing on top.

QUINOA BOWLS
WITH BRAISED RED CABBAGE, TOFU, AND BRUSSELS SPROUTS

I love serving the braised red cabbage in these autumnal bowls to friends; in my experience, it can win over even self-proclaimed cabbage haters. Sweet, sour, and salty, it's a perfect side dish for fall. In these bowls, it's paired with nutty quinoa, smoked or baked tofu, and brussels sprouts steamed until crisp-tender. If you prefer to roast the brussels sprouts, that's fine—you can do so while the cabbage braises and the quinoa cooks.

MAKES 4 BOWLS

BRAISED CABBAGE

2 teaspoons olive oil

1 white or red onion, thinly sliced

2 teaspoons sugar

½ teaspoon salt

2 tablespoons apple cider vinegar

1 small red cabbage, thinly sliced

1 apple, thinly sliced

½ cup (120 ml) water

Freshly ground black pepper

BOWLS

1 cup (170 g) quinoa, rinsed

1 pound (450 g) brussels sprouts, trimmed and halved

4 cups (120 g) firmly packed baby arugula or spinach

8 ounces (225 g) smoked or baked tofu, diced

½ cup (120 ml) Maple Mustard Dressing (see page 69)

To prepare the cabbage, heat the oil in a large skillet or pot over medium heat. Add the onion and sugar and cook, stirring occasionally, for 8 minutes, until very tender and golden brown. Stir in the salt, vinegar, cabbage, apple, and water. When the water begins to boil, lower the heat, cover, and simmer for about 30 minutes, until the cabbage is very tender, stirring a few times during cooking and adding a splash of water if the mixture gets dry or starts to stick. Season with pepper, then taste and adjust the seasonings if desired.

Meanwhile, prepare the remaining ingredients. Cook the quinoa as directed on page 13.

Pour an inch or two (2.5 or 5 cm) of water into a medium pot and insert a steamer. Bring to a boil over medium-high heat. Add the brussels sprouts, cover, and steam for 6 to 8 minutes, until bright green and tender.

To serve, divide the greens among four bowls and top each with one-quarter of the quinoa, brussels sprouts, tofu, and cabbage. Drizzle generously with the dressing and serve right away.

HARVEST BOWLS
WITH SPELT BERRIES, CIDER-GLAZED TEMPEH, AND ROASTED ROOT VEGETABLES

These bowls are all things fall: roasted root vegetables, earthy grains, maple dressing, and, my favorite component, tempeh infused with apple cider and Dijon mustard. Using cider as a marinade is both a seasonal touch and a great way to add sweetness to the tempeh without making it overly syrupy. As for the root vegetables, use a mixture of whichever types you like: parsnips, carrots, beets, rutabagas, onion, sweet potatoes, or celery root. Winter squashes, such as butternut or kabocha, also work well here.

MAKES 4 BOWLS

1 cup (about 200 g) spelt or wheat berries, barley, or farro

TEMPEH

8 ounces (225 g) tempeh, cut into ½-inch (1.3-cm) strips

1 cup (240 ml) apple cider

2 tablespoons Dijon mustard

2 tablespoons tamari

2 cloves garlic, minced or finely grated

ROASTED ROOT VEGETABLES

2 pounds (900 g) root vegetables, peeled if need be and cut into 1-inch (2.5-cm) pieces

2 tablespoons neutral vegetable oil

8 sprigs thyme

8 sprigs rosemary

Coarse salt and freshly ground black pepper

4 cups (120 g) firmly packed baby kale, spinach, or arugula

½ cup (120 ml) Maple Mustard Dressing (page 69)

Preheat the oven to 400°F (200°C), oil a 9-inch (23-cm) square baking pan, and line a rimmed baking sheet with parchment paper. Cook the spelt or other grain as directed on pages 12 to 13.

Meanwhile, prepare the tempeh. Put the strips in the oiled pan. In a small bowl or measuring cup, whisk together the cider, mustard, tamari, and garlic. Pour the mixture over the tempeh and cover the pan with foil.

To cook the root vegetables, put them in a large bowl, drizzle with the oil, and toss until evenly coated. Spread them evenly on the lined baking sheet (you may need two baking sheets) and nestle the herb sprigs among them. Sprinkle generously with salt and pepper.

Bake both the tempeh and the root vegetables for 25 minutes. Remove the foil from the tempeh and stir the vegetables well, then bake for another 20 minutes or so, until the tempeh is browning and the vegetables are tender; there will be some marinade left in the tempeh pan, but it should have thickened up considerably. If it hasn't, bake the tempeh for 5 to 10 more minutes.

To serve, divide the greens among four bowls and top each with one-quarter of the grain, tempeh, and root vegetables. Drizzle with the dressing and serve right away.

1 cup (200 g) pearl barley or farro

ROASTED PORTOBELLOS

2 large or 4 small portobello mushrooms, stemmed

2 tablespoons balsamic vinegar

1 tablespoon tamari

1 tablespoon olive oil

2 teaspoons maple syrup

2 cloves garlic, minced

SPICY BAKED TOFU

1½ tablespoons sriracha sauce or gochujang, or 2 teaspoons chili powder

2 tablespoons tomato paste

2 teaspoons agave nectar or maple syrup

1½ tablespoons rice vinegar

½ teaspoon salt

1 (15-oz, or 425-g) block extra-firm tofu, preferably pressed (see page 15), cut into 1-inch (2.5-cm) cubes

SPICY MISO DRESSING

2 tablespoons white miso

2 tablespoons warm water

2 tablespoons almond butter

2 tablespoons rice vinegar

1 tablespoon tamari

1 tablespoon agave nectar or maple syrup

1 tablespoon sriracha sauce or gochujang

1 small clove garlic (optional), minced or finely grated

4 cups (120 g) firmly packed baby spinach

OPTIONAL TOPPINGS

Steamed broccoli; toasted nuts; nutritional yeast; kimchi or sauerkraut

UMAMI BOWLS
WITH ROASTED PORTOBELLOS, TOFU, AND SPICY MISO DRESSING

My love of that distinctive fifth flavor, umami, may help explain my obsession with tomatoes, fermented foods, and mushrooms—all great sources of umami—as well as my tendency to put nutritional yeast on just about anything. Umami is on full and glorious display in these bowls, which feature marinated portobello mushrooms, spicy baked tofu, and a miso dressing spiked with sriracha sauce or gochujang. Feel free to up the umami flavor even further by adding a sprinkling of nutritional yeast, a heap of kimchi or sauerkraut, or sun-dried tomatoes.

Cook the barley as directed on page 12.

Meanwhile, preheat the oven to 425°F (220°C) and line two rimmed baking sheets with parchment paper. Put the portobellos in a shallow glass bowl. In a small bowl, whisk together the vinegar, tamari, oil, maple syrup, and garlic. Pour the mixture over the portobellos, then flip them to coat both sides. Transfer the mushrooms to one of the baking sheets, and discard the extra marinade.

To prepare the tofu, combine the sriracha sauce, tomato paste, agave nectar, vinegar, and salt in a medium bowl and whisk to combine. Add the tofu and stir gently until evenly coated. Spread the tofu on the other lined baking sheet and drizzle it with any marinade remaining in the bowl.

Bake both the tofu and the portobellos for about 35 minutes, until the edges of the tofu are crisp and the mushrooms are tender; stir the tofu once halfway through the baking time.

Meanwhile, to make the dressing, combine the miso and water in a small bowl or measuring cup and stir to create a slurry. Add the almond butter, vinegar, tamari, agave nectar, sriracha sauce, and garlic and stir or whisk until evenly combined. (Stored in an airtight container in the refrigerator, the dressing will keep for 1 week.)

Before assembling the bowls, slice the mushrooms into strips. To serve, divide the spinach among four bowls, then top each with one-quarter of the barley, portobellos, and tofu. Drizzle with the dressing and serve right away, with any other toppings you like.

GOLDEN RICE BOWLS
WITH TOFU PANEER AND VEGETABLES

Tofu paneer might sound like a stretch, but the tart, salty cubes of marinated tofu in this recipe are surprisingly authentic. Soaking the tofu in a marinade of lemon juice and nutritional yeast gives it the acidity and umami it needs to stand in for paneer. The tofu is a perfect complement to the fragrant spiced rice and vegetables in this dish, which are reminiscent of biryani. The final touch is a dressing with curry powder and goji berries that's not only delicious but also an electric, red-orange color. Goji berries can be tricky to find, so you can substitute golden raisins for a less vibrant, but equally tasty, sauce.

———————————————————

To prepare the tofu, put the cubes in a shallow glass bowl or container, preferably one large enough to fit all the tofu in a single layer. In a small bowl or measuring cup, whisk together the lemon juice, water, nutritional yeast, and salt. Pour the mixture over the tofu and stir gently until evenly coated. Cover and refrigerate for at least 8 hours and up to 12 hours.

When you're ready to prepare the bowls, preheat the oven to 400°F (200°C) and line a rimmed baking sheet with parchment paper. Spread the tofu on the lined baking sheet in a single layer and bake for 30 to 35 minutes, until golden and crispy, flipping the tofu halfway through the baking time.

Meanwhile, prepare the rice. Heat the oil in a medium pot over medium heat. Add the rice and cook, stirring constantly, for 2 to 3 minutes, until the rice smells nutty and toasted. Stir in the water, turmeric, cumin, curry powder, raisins, and salt. Bring to a boil over medium-high heat, then lower the heat, cover, and simmer for 15 minutes, until all of the liquid has been absorbed. Remove from the heat, fluff the rice gently with a fork, cover, and let sit.

CONTINUED

MAKES 4 BOWLS, AND ABOUT ¾ CUP (175 ML) OF DRESSING

TOFU PANEER

1 (15-oz, or 425-g) block extra-firm tofu, preferably pressed (see page 15), cut into ¾-inch (2-cm) cubes

3 tablespoons freshly squeezed lemon juice

2 tablespoons water

3 tablespoons nutritional yeast

½ teaspoon salt

RICE

2 teaspoons coconut oil

¾ cup (140 g) white basmati rice, rinsed

1½ cups (355 ml) water

1 teaspoon ground turmeric

½ teaspoon ground cumin

½ teaspoon curry powder

¼ cup (35 g) golden raisins

¼ teaspoon salt

VEGETABLES

1 tablespoon coconut oil

½ white or yellow onion, chopped

2 cloves garlic, minced

1 teaspoon minced fresh ginger

2 cups (215 g) cauliflower florets

3½ ounces (100 g) green beans, trimmed and cut into 1-inch (2.5-cm) pieces

1 cup (140 g) fresh or frozen green peas

1 cup (110 g) grated carrots (about 2 carrots)

¼ teaspoon salt

¾ cup (175 ml) water

Freshly ground black pepper

GOJI CURRY DRESSING

¼ cup (30 g) raw cashews, soaked for at least 2 hours and drained

2 heaping tablespoons goji berries, soaked for at least 2 hours and drained

¼ cup (60 ml) water

2 tablespoons freshly squeezed lime juice

1 clove garlic, chopped

¼ teaspoon salt

1 teaspoon curry powder

¼ cup (about 25 g) sliced or slivered almonds, toasted

To cook the vegetables, heat the oil in a large skillet over medium-high heat. Add the onion and cook, stirring occasionally, for 5 minutes, until tender and translucent. Add the garlic and ginger and cook, stirring constantly, for 1 minute. Add the cauliflower, green beans, peas, carrots, salt, and water, then season with pepper. Bring to a simmer, then lower the heat, cover, and simmer for about 10 minutes, until all of the vegetables are fork-tender.

To make the dressing, combine all the ingredients in a blender (preferably a high-speed blender) and process until smooth. (Stored in an airtight container in the refrigerator, the dressing will keep for 5 days.)

To assemble the bowls, first stir the rice into the vegetables. Taste and adjust the seasonings if desired. Divide the rice and vegetables among four bowls. Scatter the tofu paneer on top, then sprinkle with the almonds and drizzle with the dressing. Serve right away.

SWEET POTATOES

3 medium sweet potatoes, scrubbed and diced

1½ tablespoons neutral vegetable oil

½ teaspoon smoked paprika

1 teaspoon ground cumin

½ teaspoon coarse salt

⅛ teaspoon cayenne pepper

RICE

2 teaspoons coconut oil

1 cup (185 g) white or brown basmati rice, rinsed

2 cups (475 ml) water

1 teaspoon finely grated lime zest

1 tablespoon freshly squeezed lime juice

¼ teaspoon salt

¼ cup (10 g) chopped fresh cilantro

BLACK BEANS

1½ cups (270 g) cooked black beans, or 1 (15-oz, or 425-g) can, drained and rinsed

2 tablespoons finely chopped red onion

1 small jalapeño chile, seeded and finely chopped

Pinch of ground cumin

1 to 2 tablespoons freshly squeezed lime juice

1 small Hass avocado, pitted, peeled, and chopped

Salt and freshly ground black pepper

BOWLS

5 cups (150 g) firmly packed baby greens, such as spinach, arugula, or romaine

Hemp Chimichurri Sauce (see page 178) or Cashew Queso Sauce (see page 225), for drizzling

SWEET POTATO BOWLS
WITH CILANTRO LIME RICE AND BLACK BEANS

I love every part of this dish: the spice-rubbed sweet potatoes, the rice flecked with lime zest and cilantro, and the tangy black beans enhanced with creamy avocado. When served over fresh greens, they add up to a perfect summer meal.

To prepare the sweet potatoes, preheat the oven to 400°F (200°C) and line a rimmed baking sheet with parchment paper. In a large bowl, toss the sweet potatoes with the oil until evenly coated. Sprinkle with the paprika and cumin, season with salt and cayenne, and toss again. Spread the sweet potatoes evenly on the lined baking sheet and bake for 30 to 35 minutes, until tender and browning at the edges.

Meanwhile, to make the rice, heat 1 teaspoon of the oil in a medium pot over medium-low heat. Add the rice and cook, stirring constantly, for 2 to 3 minutes, until the rice smells nutty and toasted. Stir in the water and bring to a boil over medium-high heat. Lower the heat, cover, and simmer for about 15 minutes for white basmati or about 40 minutes for brown basmati, until all of the liquid has been absorbed. Remove from heat and stir in the remaining 1 teaspoon coconut oil, the lime zest and juice, and the salt. Fold in the cilantro just before serving.

To prepare the black beans, put all of the ingredients in a medium bowl and stir gently to combine. Taste and adjust the seasonings if desired.

To serve, divide the greens among four bowls and top each with one-quarter of the sweet potatoes, rice, and bean mixture. Drizzle with the chimichurri sauce and serve right away.

SUSHI BOWLS

This bowl is a perfect example of how the right combination of simple ingredients can add up to a bold and memorable meal (especially when there's a great sauce involved). Feel free to get playful with your toppings and ingredients: you can substitute steamed edamame for the tofu, vary the vegetables depending on what's in season or what you have in your fridge, or substitute Spicy Miso Dressing (see page 139) for the Sriracha Mayonnaise. I like to garnish my bowls with pickled ginger or *gomasio*, a traditional Japanese condiment made from toasted sesame seeds and sea salt.

_____

MAKES 4 BOWLS, AND ABOUT ½ CUP (120 ML) OF SRIRACHA MAYONNAISE

SRIRACHA MAYONNAISE

⅓ cup (80 g) vegan mayonnaise

1 tablespoon rice vinegar

2 tablespoons sriracha sauce

1 small clove garlic (optional), minced or finely grated

2 teaspoons tamari

Red pepper flakes (optional)

BOWLS

1 cup (200 g) short-grain brown rice

8 ounces (225 g) smoked or baked tofu, cubed

2 cucumbers, peeled and chopped or sliced into strips with a julienne peeler

4 carrots, peeled and grated or sliced into thin strips with a julienne peeler

2 cups (140 g) finely shredded red or green cabbage

1 Hass avocado, pitted, peeled, and sliced

4 large sheets toasted nori, cut into thin strips

OPTIONAL TOPPINGS

Additional vegetables (steamed or raw), pickled ginger, toasted sesame seeds or gomasio, gochujang or sriracha sauce, chopped scallions, wasabi

To prepare the mayonnaise, combine all the ingredients in a small bowl and whisk until well blended. Taste and adjust the seasonings if desired. (Stored in an airtight container in the refrigerator, the mayonnaise will keep for 1 week.)

Cook the rice as directed on page 13.

To serve, divide the rice among four bowls. Top each with one-quarter of the tofu, cucumbers, carrots, cabbage, avocado, and nori, then drizzle with the mayonnaise. Serve right away, with any additional toppings you like.

FENNEL

2 large bulbs fennel, sliced
lengthwise ¼ inch (6 mm) thick

1 tablespoon olive oil

Coarse salt and freshly ground
black pepper

QUINOA

1 cup (170 g) quinoa, rinsed

2 tablespoons olive oil

2 tablespoons freshly squeezed
lemon juice

2 teaspoons red wine vinegar

2 teaspoons chopped fresh
oregano leaves, or ½ teaspoon
dried oregano

1 clove garlic, minced

¼ teaspoon salt

1½ cups (250 g) cooked black-
eyed peas, or 1 (15-oz, or
425-g) can, drained and rinsed

1 small cucumber, peeled
and chopped

1 cup (150 g) cherry tomatoes,
halved

⅓ cup (13 g) chopped fresh
parsley

¼ cup (10 g) chopped fresh mint
leaves

SMOKED PAPRIKA HUMMUS

1½ cups (250 grams) cooked
chickpeas, or 1 (15-oz, or
425-g) can, drained and rinsed

½ teaspoon salt

½ teaspoon ground cumin

½ teaspoon smoked paprika

2 tablespoons freshly squeezed
lemon juice

1 clove garlic, chopped

¼ cup (60 grams) tahini

¼ cup (60 ml) water, plus more
if needed

Freshly ground black pepper

MEDITERRANEAN QUINOA BOWLS
WITH ROASTED FENNEL AND BLACK-EYED PEAS

I use a lot of Mediterranean-inspired ingredients and seasonings at
home, especially tomato, cucumber, lemon, and oregano (I am half
Greek, after all). Although black-eyed peas are often associated
with Southern cuisine, they're actually a common legume in Greek
cooking, and their subtle nuttiness is a nice complement to sweet
roasted fennel. I call for topping these bowls with Smoked Paprika
Hummus, but you could substitute Everyday Lemon Tahini Dressing
(see page 66)—or use both!

To prepare the fennel, preheat the oven to 400°F (200°C) and line
a rimmed baking sheet with parchment paper. In a large bowl, toss
the fennel with the oil until evenly coated. Spread it on the lined
baking sheet and sprinkle with salt and pepper. Bake for 30 to
35 minutes, until very tender and golden brown, stirring once
halfway through the baking time.

Meanwhile, cook the quinoa as directed on page 13.

In a small bowl or measuring cup, combine the oil, lemon juice,
vinegar, oregano, garlic, and salt and whisk until evenly combined.

Transfer the quinoa to a large bowl. Add the black-eyed peas,
cucumber, tomatoes, parsley, and mint, then pour in the dressing
and stir gently until well combined.

To make the hummus, combine the chickpeas, salt, cumin,
paprika, lemon juice, garlic, and tahini in a food processor and
pulse for about 15 seconds. With the motor running, add the
water in a thin stream and process for about 1 minute. Scrape
down the sides of the work bowl, then process for another
minute, until very smooth and creamy, adding more water if
needed to achieve the desired consistency. Season with pepper,
then taste and adjust the seasonings if desired.

To serve, divide the quinoa mixture among four bowls and top
each with one-quarter of the fennel and hummus. Serve right away.

THAI PEANUT NOODLE BOWLS
WITH SPICY LIME TOFU AND CRISP VEGETABLES

MAKES 4 BOWLS

TOFU

1 (15-oz, or 425-g) block extra-firm tofu, preferably pressed (see page 15), cut into 1-inch (2.5-cm) cubes

3 tablespoons tamari

1 tablespoon neutral vegetable oil

Finely grated zest of 1 lime

3 tablespoons freshly squeezed lime juice

3 cloves garlic, minced

½ teaspoon red pepper flakes, plus more if desired

SAUCE

5 tablespoons (80 g) smooth peanut butter

⅓ cup (80 ml) hot water

2 tablespoons red curry paste, plus more if desired

1 tablespoon tamari

1 clove garlic, minced

2 teaspoons maple syrup or agave nectar

3 tablespoons freshly squeezed lime juice

BOWLS

2 cups (180 g) bite-size broccoli florets

2 cups (200 g) snow peas or sugar snap peas

7 ounces (200 g) asparagus, trimmed and cut into 1-inch (2.5-cm) pieces

8 ounces (225 g) soba noodles

OPTIONAL TOPPINGS

Chopped roasted peanuts or cashews, sriracha sauce, chopped scallions, chopped fresh basil, cilantro, or mint leaves

There's something magical about the combination of Thai curry paste and peanut butter, and that magic is on full display in these flavorful noodle bowls. The tart and spicy tofu cubes are great not just in this recipe but also in salads and on rice; however, you can substitute store-bought baked tofu (preferably an Asian-inspired flavor) if you're short on time.

To prepare the tofu, put the cubes in a shallow glass bowl or container, preferably one large enough to fit all of the tofu in a single layer. In a small bowl, whisk together the tamari, oil, lime zest and juice, garlic, and red pepper flakes. Pour the mixture over the tofu and stir gently to evenly coat the tofu. Let sit for at least 20 minutes, or cover and refrigerate for up to 12 hours.

Preheat the oven to 400°F (200°C) and line a rimmed baking sheet with parchment paper. Remove the tofu from the marinade and spread it in a single layer on the lined baking sheet (discard any remaining marinade). Bake for 25 to 30 minutes, until crispy, flipping the tofu once halfway through the baking time.

Meanwhile, to make the sauce, combine all the ingredients in a small bowl and whisk until evenly blended.

To prepare the remaining ingredients, bring a large pot of water to a boil over high heat. Add the broccoli and blanch for 1 minute. Add the snow peas and asparagus and blanch for 1 to 2 minutes, until all of the vegetables are crisp-tender. Use a slotted spoon to transfer the vegetables to a colander to drain completely.

Add the soba noodles to the same boiling water, then adjust the heat to maintain a low boil. Cook, stirring occasionally, until the noodles are tender but still firm, then drain the soba well and transfer to a large bowl. Add about three-quarters of the sauce and stir gently to combine.

To serve, divide the noodles among four bowls and top each with one-quarter of the vegetables and tofu, then drizzle with the remaining sauce. Serve right away, with any other desired toppings.

MILLET PILAF BOWLS
WITH BARBECUE TOFU AND BRAISED COLLARD GREENS

MAKES 4 BOWLS

TOFU

1 (8-oz, or 227-g) can tomato sauce

1 tablespoon maple syrup

1 tablespoon blackstrap molasses

1 tablespoon apple cider vinegar

1 tablespoon tamari

1 tablespoon Dijon mustard

½ teaspoon smoked paprika

1½ teaspoons chili powder

Pinch of cayenne pepper

1 (15-oz, or 425-g) block extra-firm tofu, preferably pressed (see page 15), cut into 8 equal rectangles

MILLET PILAF

1 tablespoon olive oil

1 small white or yellow onion, chopped

2 carrots, peeled and diced

1 cup (220 g) millet, rinsed

2 cloves garlic, finely minced

2 cups (475 ml) low-sodium vegetable broth

½ teaspoon salt

⅓ cup (about 35 g) sliced or slivered almonds, toasted

COLLARD GREENS

1 tablespoon olive oil

3 cloves garlic, thinly sliced

1 bunch collard greens, stemmed and cut into thin strips

½ cup (120 ml) low-sodium vegetable broth

¼ teaspoon smoked paprika

½ teaspoon salt

Freshly ground black pepper

There's no better way to give tofu mainstream appeal than to marinate it in homemade barbecue sauce and then bake or grill it. Barbecue tofu gets star billing in these bowls, but I'm also partial to the millet pilaf, which one friend has told me reminds her of cornbread in a whole grain form!

To prepare the tofu, preheat the oven to 350°F (175°C) and oil an 8- or 9-inch (20- or 23-cm) square baking pan. In a small bowl, whisk together the tomato sauce, maple syrup, molasses, vinegar, tamari, mustard, paprika, chili powder, and cayenne. Pour about half of this barbecue sauce into the oiled pan. Lay the tofu pieces on top and spread the rest of the barbecue sauce over the tofu. Cover the pan with foil and bake for 15 minutes. Remove the foil and bake for 15 to 20 minutes, until the sauce is dark, bubbly, and quite thick.

Meanwhile, to make the pilaf, heat the oil in a medium pot over medium heat. Add the onion and carrots and cook, stirring occasionally, for 5 to 7 minutes, until the onion is translucent and the carrots are tender. Add the millet and garlic and cook, stirring constantly, for about 2 minutes, until the garlic is fragrant and the millet smells a bit nutty. Stir in the broth and salt and bring to a boil over medium-high heat. Lower the heat, cover, and simmer for about 20 minutes, until the broth has been absorbed. Gently fold in the almonds. Taste and adjust the seasonings if desired.

While the pilaf is cooking, prepare the collard greens. Heat the oil in a large skillet over medium heat. Add the garlic and let sizzle for about 1 minute, until just beginning to brown, stirring gently to prevent burning. Add the collard greens and broth, cover, and cook for about 1 minute. Stir in the paprika and salt and cook, stirring frequently, for 7 to 10 minutes, until the collard greens are tender. Season with pepper, then taste and adjust the seasonings if desired.

To assemble the bowls, divide the millet pilaf among four bowls and top each with one-quarter of the tofu and collard greens. Dollop any barbecue sauce remaining in the baking pan on top and serve right away.

KOREAN TEMPEH BOWLS
WITH BROCCOLI AND BROWN RICE

MAKES 4 BOWLS

1 cup (200 g) short-grain brown rice

TEMPEH

8 ounces (225 g) tempeh, cut into ¾-inch (2-cm) cubes

¼ cup (60 ml) tamari

3 tablespoons rice vinegar

2 tablespoons mirin, or 1 tablespoon rice vinegar plus 1 teaspoon sugar

1½ tablespoons toasted sesame oil

1 tablespoon sugar

4 cloves garlic, finely minced or grated

1 tablespoon finely minced or grated fresh ginger

1 to 2 teaspoons red pepper flakes

1 tablespoon neutral vegetable oil

VEGETABLES

1½ teaspoons neutral vegetable oil

2 large carrots, peeled and cut into matchsticks or sliced into long strips with a julienne peeler

2 small zucchini, cut into matchsticks or sliced into long strips with a julienne peeler

10 to 12 ounces (285 to 340 g) broccoli, cut into bite-size pieces

1 cup (35 g) bean sprouts (optional)

5 ounces (140 g) kimchi

2 tablespoons toasted sesame seeds

OPTIONAL TOPPINGS

Red pepper flakes, sriracha sauce or gochujang; chopped scallions; peanuts; Sriracha Mayonnaise (see page 146)

At the center of this dish is a vegan spin on the popular Korean *bulgogi*, grilled, marinated beef slices. Tempeh takes its place ably, adding protein, texture, and heft to these bowls, while sautéed vegetables and kimchi add color.

Cook the rice as directed on page 13.

To prepare the tempeh, put the cubes in a shallow glass bowl or container, preferably one large enough to fit all the tempeh in a single layer. In a small bowl or measuring cup, whisk together the tamari, vinegar, mirin, toasted sesame oil, sugar, garlic, ginger, and red pepper flakes (1 teaspoon red pepper flakes if you want a little heat, 2 teaspoons if you want it spicy). Pour the mixture over the tempeh and stir gently to evenly coat. Cover and let sit until the rice is cooked.

Heat the vegetable oil in a large skillet over medium heat. Remove the tempeh from the marinade, reserving the marinade, and put it in the skillet. Cook, flipping the tempeh frequently, for 7 to 8 minutes, until browned on all sides. Transfer the tempeh to a plate or small bowl.

To cook the vegetables, heat the oil in the same skillet over medium heat. Add the carrots, zucchini, broccoli, and bean sprouts and cook, stirring frequently, for about 3 minutes, until the broccoli is bright green and the carrots are becoming tender. Lower the heat to low, add the reserved marinade, and cook, stirring frequently, for 3 to 5 minutes, until the broccoli is crisp-tender.

To serve, divide the rice evenly among four bowls and top each with one-quarter of the tempeh, vegetables, and kimchi. Sprinkle with the sesame seeds and serve right away, with any other desired toppings.

MACRO BOWLS
WITH ADZUKI BEANS AND MISO-GLAZED KABOCHA SQUASH

MAKES 4 BOWLS, AND ABOUT
¾ CUP (175 ML) OF DRESSING

RICE

1 cup (200 g) short-grain
brown rice

1 teaspoon toasted sesame oil

1 tablespoon toasted sesame
seeds

1 scallion, green part only, very
thinly sliced

1 tablespoon mirin (optional)

SQUASH

1 tablespoon neutral vegetable oil

1 tablespoon white miso

1 tablespoon tamari

1 tablespoon mirin (optional)

1 pound (450 g) kabocha squash,
seeded and cut into 1-inch
(2.5-cm) pieces

DRESSING

¼ cup (60 g) tahini

2 tablespoons white miso

1 tablespoon rice vinegar

1 tablespoon freshly squeezed
lemon juice

1 tablespoon agave nectar or
maple syrup

2 teaspoons toasted sesame oil

2 teaspoons finely grated or
minced fresh ginger

¼ cup (60 ml) warm water, plus
more if needed

BOWLS

1 bunch curly kale, stemmed and
torn into pieces

1½ cups (345 g) cooked adzuki
beans, or 1 (15-oz, or 425-g) can,
drained and rinsed

1 cup (240 ml) fermented
vegetables, such as kimchi
or sauerkraut

It's no surprise that I have a weakness for macro plates. These dishes, the cornerstone of macrobiotic cookery, are focused on the idea of macronutrient balance, and they feature a balanced ratio of beans, grains, and vegetables. My version takes some liberties (I haven't been able to perfect the traditional sea vegetable salad at home), but it does feature the signature kabocha squash—kicked up with a miso glaze—as well as the traditional rice, beans, greens, and a sweet and salty miso-based dressing. Top with toasted nori strips, chopped scallions, and toasted sesame seeds, as you like.

Cook the rice as directed on page 13. Drizzle the cooked rice with the sesame oil, then gently fold in the sesame seeds, scallion, and mirin.

While the rice is cooking, prepare the squash. Preheat the oven to 400°F (200°C) and line a rimmed baking sheet with parchment paper. In a small bowl or measuring cup, whisk together the oil, miso, tamari, and mirin. Put the squash in a large bowl, drizzle with the miso mixture, and toss until evenly coated. Spread the squash on the lined baking sheet in a single layer and bake for 20 minutes, until tender and browning at the edges.

Meanwhile, to make the dressing, combine all the ingredients in a small bowl or measuring cup and whisk until smooth. If it's thicker than you'd like, whisk in additional warm water, 1 tablespoon at a time, to achieve the desired consistency.

Before assembling the bowls, pour an inch or two (2.5 or 5 cm) of water into a medium pot and insert a steamer. Bring to a boil over medium-high heat. Add the kale and steam for about 3 minutes, until bright green and tender.

To serve, divide the rice, squash, kale, and adzuki beans among four bowls. Top each with one-quarter of the fermented vegetables and drizzle generously with the dressing. Serve right away.

GREEN GODDESS BOWLS

MAKES 4 BOWLS, AND ABOUT
1 CUP (240 ML) OF DRESSING

FARRO PILAF

1 cup (200 g) pearl or hulled farro

1½ cups (250 g) cooked chickpeas, or 1 (15-oz, or 425-g) can, drained and rinsed

1 small stalk celery, finely chopped

2 scallions, green parts only, chopped

2 tablespoons chopped fresh dill, or 2 teaspoons dried dill weed

1 tablespoon olive oil

2 teaspoons freshly squeezed lemon juice

Salt and freshly ground black pepper

TAHINI GREEN GODDESS DRESSING

5 tablespoons (75 ml) water

¼ cup (60 g) tahini

1 tablespoon freshly squeezed lemon juice

1 tablespoon apple cider vinegar

1 tablespoon agave nectar or maple syrup

1 clove garlic, coarsely chopped

¼ cup (10 g) coarsely chopped fresh parsley

¼ cup (10 g) coarsely chopped fresh basil leaves

1 scallion, green part only, chopped

½ teaspoon salt

Freshly ground black pepper

BOWLS

10 to 12 ounces (285 to 340 g) broccoli, cut into bite-size pieces

4 cups (120 g) firmly packed baby spinach

1 large or 2 small Hass avocados, peeled, pitted, and sliced

Sometimes, especially after lots of recipe testing or holiday cooking, I crave a simple bowl of something green. That's when this recipe hits the spot. There's nothing super fancy here: just fresh greens, steamed broccoli, lightly dressed chickpeas and farro, creamy avocado, and—the kicker—a green goddess dressing that's practically drinkable. I like farro in this recipe because its density is a nice counterpart to all of the greenery and crunch, but feel free to substitute short-grain brown rice or any other cooked whole grain.

To make the pilaf, cook the farro as directed on page 13. Transfer to a medium bowl, add the chickpeas, celery, scallions, dill, oil, and lemon juice, and stir gently until well combined. Season with salt and pepper to taste.

To make the dressing, combine all the ingredients in a blender and process until smooth. (Stored in an airtight container in the refrigerator, the dressing will keep for 4 to 5 days.)

Before assembling the bowls, pour an inch or two (2.5 or 5 cm) of water into a medium pot and insert a steamer. Bring to a boil over medium-high heat. Add the broccoli and steam for 3 to 5 minutes, until tender. Drain well.

To serve, divide the baby spinach among four bowls. Top each with one-quarter of the farro, broccoli, and avocado. Drizzle with the dressing and serve right away.

FALAFEL

1 large sweet potato, cooked, flesh scooped out and mashed (about 1 cup, or 245 g)

1½ cups (250 g) cooked chickpeas, or 1 (15-oz, or 425-g) can, drained and rinsed

1 clove garlic, chopped

½ cup (15 g) loosely packed fresh parsley

¼ cup (30 g) chickpea flour

1 teaspoon ground flaxseed

1 teaspoon ground cumin

½ teaspoon smoked paprika

½ teaspoon salt

¼ teaspoon freshly ground black pepper

1 tablespoon freshly squeezed lemon juice

CAULIFLOWER

1 medium head cauliflower, cut into bite-size pieces

1 tablespoon olive oil

2 teaspoons grated lemon zest

Coarse salt and freshly ground black pepper

FREEKEH PILAF

1 tablespoon olive oil

1 small onion, chopped

2 carrots, peeled and diced

1 cup (200 g) freekeh, rinsed

¼ teaspoon salt

2½ cups (590 ml) low-sodium vegetable broth

Freshly ground black pepper

BOWLS

4 cups (120 g) baby arugula

1 cup (150 g) cherry tomatoes, quartered, or 1 tomato, chopped

1 cucumber, peeled and chopped

¾ cup (175 ml) Everyday Lemon Tahini Dressing (see page 66)

SWEET POTATO FALAFEL BOWLS
WITH FREEKEH PILAF AND
ROASTED CAULIFLOWER

The stars of this dish are crispy, oven-baked sweet potato falafel, which are piled over roasted cauliflower and a nutty freekeh pilaf. Each of the components takes a bit of time to prepare, but the results are worth it: vibrant, flavorful, and complex. The freekeh and falafel can both be prepared up to 3 days in advance.

———————————————

To make the falafel, preheat the oven to 375°F (190°C) and line two rimmed baking sheets with parchment paper. In a food processor, combine the sweet potato, chickpeas, garlic, and parsley and pulse 10 to 15 times, until the chickpeas and parsley are broken down. Scrape down the sides of the work bowl, then add the chickpea flour, ground flaxseed, cumin, paprika, salt, pepper, and lemon juice and pulse 5 to 10 times, taking care not to overprocess the mixture; it should retain some texture.

Roll the mixture into 1½-inch (4-cm) balls; you should have about 16. Place the balls on one of the lined baking sheets.

To prepare the cauliflower, put it in a large bowl and toss with the oil. Sprinkle with the lemon zest and a pinch each of salt and pepper and toss again. Spread on the second baking sheet.

Bake both the falafel and cauliflower for 15 minutes, then stir the cauliflower and gently flip the falafel. Bake for about 15 minutes longer, until the falafel are crispy and the cauliflower is lightly browned.

Meanwhile, to make the pilaf, heat the oil in a medium pot over medium heat. Add the onion and carrots and cook, stirring occasionally, for 5 to 7 minutes, until the onion is translucent and the carrots are tender. Stir in the freekeh, salt, and broth and bring to a boil over medium-high heat. Lower the heat, cover, and simmer for 20 to 25 minutes, until all of the broth has been absorbed. Fluff the freekeh with a fork. Season with black pepper.

To serve, divide the arugula among four bowls and top each with one-quarter of the pilaf, cauliflower, falafel, tomatoes, and cucumber. Drizzle with the dressing and serve right away.

PROVENÇAL BOWLS
WITH LENTIL SALAD
AND HERBED CASHEW CHEESE

MAKES 4 BOWLS, AND 1 CUP
(240 ML) OF CRUMBLED CASHEW
CHEESE

3 or 4 red or golden beets, tops
trimmed

LENTIL SALAD

1 cup (200 g) dried French green
lentils

⅓ cup chopped sun-dried
tomatoes, oil-packed (40 g) or
dry-packed (20 g)

1 scallion, green part only,
chopped

1½ tablespoons capers

2 tablespoons olive oil

1½ tablespoons red wine vinegar
or champagne vinegar

2 teaspoons Dijon mustard

1 tablespoon finely chopped
shallot (optional)

½ teaspoon salt

Pinch of freshly ground black
pepper

CASHEW CHEESE

1 cup (130 g) raw cashews, soaked
for at least 2 hours and drained

2 tablespoons nutritional yeast

2 tablespoons freshly squeezed
lemon juice

1 small clove garlic, coarsely
chopped, or ⅛ teaspoon garlic
powder

½ teaspoon salt

¼ teaspoon freshly ground black
pepper

¼ cup (60 ml) water, plus more if
needed

1 tablespoon herbes de Provence,
or 1½ teaspoons each dried thyme
and dried oregano

4 cups (120 g) firmly packed
mesclun or baby arugula

"I'd go vegan, but I can't live without cheese." Every vegan has heard these words uttered by friends or family members—possibly many times over. But times are changing, and these days there are many vegan cheeses on the market, ranging from melty shredded cheeses to soft, artisanal nut cheeses. I'm thrilled to have new options, but I've been making the homemade cashew cheese in this recipe for years, and it's still one of my favorites. You can substitute any soft, crumbly vegan cheese in its place.

_____

Preheat the oven to 400°F (200°C). Wrap each beet in foil. Put them on a baking sheet and bake for about 45 minutes, until fork-tender. Remove the foil and, once the beets are cool enough to handle, rub off the skins under cold running water. Cut into wedges.

Meanwhile, to prepare the lentil salad, cook the lentils as directed on page 15. Drain, rinse under cold running water, then let drain completely. Transfer to a large bowl and stir in the sun-dried tomatoes, scallion, and capers.

In a small bowl or measuring cup, whisk together the oil, vinegar, mustard, shallot, salt, and pepper. Pour over the lentils and mix well. Taste and adjust the seasonings if desired.

To prepare the cashew cheese, combine the cashews, nutritional yeast, lemon juice, garlic, salt, and pepper in a food processor and pulse repeatedly until the cashews form a coarse, wet meal. Scrape down the sides of the work bowl. Turn on the processor and, with the motor running, add the water in a thin stream and process for about 10 seconds. Scrape down the sides of the work bowl again, then process for 1 to 2 minutes, until the cheese is smooth and thick, adding just a bit of water if needed to allow for processing. The consistency should be similar to thick hummus. Pulse in the herbes de Provence, then taste and adjust the seasonings if desired. (Stored in an airtight container in the refrigerator, the cheese will keep for 5 days.)

To serve, divide the mesclun among four bowls and top each with one-quarter of the lentil salad, beets, and cheese. Serve right away.

1 cup (170 g) quinoa, rinsed

KEFTEDES

¾ cup (150 g) dried brown or green lentils, or 1 (15-ounce, or 425-g) can lentils, drained and rinsed

⅓ cup (35 g) walnuts

⅓ cup (30 g) rolled oats

2 cloves garlic, minced or finely grated

1 teaspoon dried oregano

½ teaspoon onion powder

2 tablespoons nutritional yeast

1 tablespoon tamari

¼ cup (10 g) chopped fresh parsley

Water, if needed

TZATZIKI

1 cucumber

⅔ cup (85 g) raw cashews, soaked for at least 2 hours and drained

½ cup (120 ml) water

¼ teaspoon salt

1 clove garlic

2 tablespoons freshly squeezed lemon juice

¼ cup (8 g) chopped fresh dill

¼ cup (10 g) chopped fresh mint leaves

2 tomatoes, chopped

1 cucumber, peeled and chopped

½ cup (65 g) kalamata olives, pitted and halved

Pinch of salt

Pinch of freshly ground pepper

2 teaspoons olive oil (optional)

4 cups (120 g) firmly packed baby spinach or chopped romaine

1 (6-oz, or 170-g) jar marinated artichoke hearts, drained and chopped (optional)

GREEK BOWLS
WITH LENTIL KEFTEDES
AND CASHEW TZATZIKI

I stopped eating red meat as a kid, so it's been a long time since I tasted my yaya's *keftedes*, a traditional Greek rendition of meatballs typically made with onion, breadcrumbs, garlic, and oregano. My vegan version is prepared with lentils, oats, and walnuts in place of the meat and breadcrumbs, making it lighter and more nutritious, yet equally flavorful. My favorite way to enjoy these *keftedes* is with a generous drizzle of tangy vegan tzatziki, a classic Greek sauce made with yogurt and cucumbers.

Cook the quinoa as directed on page 13.

To make the *keftedes*, cook the lentils as directed on page 15. Drain, rinse under cold running water, then let drain completely.

Put the walnuts and oats in a food processor and process until the texture resembles coarse meal. Add the garlic, oregano, onion powder, and nutritional yeast and pulse a few times to incorporate. Add the lentils, tamari, and parsley and pulse until the ingredients are evenly mixed and clumping together; you may need to scrape down the sides of the work bowl or add a tablespoonful of water to allow for processing. Roll the mixture into 1-inch (2.5-cm) balls; you should have about 16. Put the *keftedes* on the lined baking sheet and bake for about 25 minutes, until they're starting to get crisp, flipping them gently halfway through the baking time.

Meanwhile, to make the tzatziki, peel the cucumber, then halve it, scrape out the seeds, and grate the flesh. Put the cucumber in a fine-mesh sieve and press to expel as much moisture as possible. Transfer to a medium bowl. Combine the cashews, water, salt, garlic, and lemon juice in a blender (preferably a high-speed blender) and process until smooth. Transfer to the bowl with the cucumber, add the dill and mint, and stir to combine.

Before assembling the bowls, put the tomatoes, cucumber, olives, salt, pepper, and olive oil in a bowl and stir gently until evenly combined. To serve, divide the spinach among four bowls and top each with one-quarter of the quinoa, *keftedes*, tomato and olive mixture, artichokes, and tzatziki. Serve right away.

COCONUT KALE AND LENTIL BOWLS
WITH ROASTED DELICATA SQUASH
AND JASMINE RICE

The saucy, spicy coconut kale in these bowls has won over the kale skeptics in my life. I pair it with lentils for protein and texture, as well as tender jasmine rice and sweet rings of roasted delicata squash. This is a great winter squash because the skin is so thin that it doesn't need to be peeled. If you can't find delicata squash, substitute another type of winter squash or sweet potato. I recommend serving the bowls with a drizzle of Goji Curry Dressing; it adds just the right sweet-tart finish to the dish.

Cook the rice as directed on page 14.

To prepare the squash, preheat the oven to 400°F (200°C) and line a rimmed baking sheet with parchment paper. In a large bowl, toss the squash with the oil until evenly coated. Spread the squash on the lined baking sheet and sprinkle with salt and pepper. Bake for 25 to 30 minutes, until fork-tender, flipping once halfway through the baking time.

Meanwhile, to prepare the kale and lentils, heat the oil in a large pot over medium heat. Add the onion and cook, stirring occasionally, for 5 minutes, until tender. Stir in the ginger, lentils, and broth. Bring to a boil over high heat, then lower the heat, cover, and simmer for 25 to 30 minutes, until the lentils are tender but not mushy. Add the kale, cover, and cook for 2 minutes. Stir in the kale. Add the coconut milk, lime juice, tamari, and red pepper flakes and stir well. Taste and adjust the seasonings if desired.

To serve, divide the rice among four bowls and top each with one-quarter of the squash and the kale and lentils. Drizzle with the dressing and serve right away.

MAKES 4 BOWLS

1 cup (185 g) white jasmine or basmati rice

SQUASH

1¾ pounds (800 g) delicata squash, seeded and cut into rings ½ inch (1.3 cm) thick

1 tablespoon melted coconut oil

Salt and freshly ground black pepper

KALE AND LENTILS

1 tablespoon coconut oil

1 small white or yellow onion, diced

1 tablespoon finely grated or minced fresh ginger

¾ cup (150 g) dried brown, green, or black lentils

2¾ cups (650 ml) low-sodium vegetable broth

1 bunch kale, stemmed and torn into bite-size pieces

½ cup (120 ml) full-fat coconut milk

2 tablespoons freshly squeezed lime juice

1 tablespoon tamari

Pinch of red pepper flakes

¾ cup (175 ml) Goji Curry Dressing (optional; see page 142)

DELI BOWLS
WITH SMASHED CHICKPEA SALAD

MAKES 4 BOWLS

CHICKPEA SALAD

3 cups (500 g) cooked chickpeas, or 2 (15-oz, or 425-g) cans, drained and rinsed

2 stalks celery, finely chopped

2 scallions, green parts only, chopped

1 large dill pickle, finely chopped

2 tablespoons chopped fresh dill, or 2 teaspoons dried dill weed

1 tablespoon capers (optional)

6 tablespoons (90 g) vegan mayonnaise or tahini, plus more if needed

1 tablespoon apple cider vinegar

1½ tablespoons Dijon mustard

¼ teaspoon salt

Freshly ground black pepper

BOWLS

5 cups (150 g) firmly packed baby spinach, baby arugula, or chopped lettuce

2 cups (300 g) cherry tomatoes, halved or quartered

1 large cucumber, peeled and chopped

1 cup (240 ml) Tahini Green Goddess Dressing (see page 158), or ¾ cup (175 ml) Everyday Lemon Tahini Dressing (see page 66)

4 whole wheat pita breads, cut into quarters, or 4 slices rye, pumpernickel, or sourdough toast, cut into quarters

OPTIONAL TOPPINGS

Chopped dill pickles, sauerkraut, pickled beets, chopped scallions

These deli bowls are easy, satisfying, and, unlike all of the other recipes in this chapter, require no cooking at all. They're a perfect option for a casual lunch. The chickpea salad, which is reminiscent of chicken salad, is a staple in my home. I use it on sandwiches, in wraps, or with crackers for a tasty snack. The grain in this bowl is pita bread, but you could certainly substitute a cooked whole grain if you like.

———————————————

To make the chickpea salad, put the chickpeas into a large bowl and use a potato masher or a fork to mash them partially, leaving about half of the chickpeas whole. Add the celery, scallions, pickle, dill, capers, mayonnaise, vinegar, mustard, and salt and mix well. Add a bit more mayonnaise if needed to hold the mixture together. Season with pepper, then taste and adjust the seasonings. Toast the pita, if desired.

To serve, divide the lettuce, tomatoes, and cucumber among four bowls. Drizzle with the dressing and top with the pita wedges and one-quarter of the chickpea salad. Serve right away, offering any other desired toppings at the table.

MARRAKECH BOWLS
WITH HARISSA-ROASTED VEGETABLES
AND BULGUR PILAF

MAKES 4 SERVINGS

VEGETABLES AND CHICKPEAS

4 carrots, peeled and cut into
1-inch (2.5-cm) pieces

4 parsnips, peeled and cut into
1-inch (2.5-cm) pieces

1 large red or yellow beet, peeled
and diced

1 red onion, cut into wedges

1½ cups (250 g) cooked chickpeas,
or 1 (15-oz, or 425-g) can, drained
and rinsed

2 tablespoons olive oil

1 teaspoon fennel seeds

1 teaspoon cumin seeds, or
½ teaspoon ground cumin

1 teaspoon sweet paprika

1 tablespoon harissa paste, or
1 teaspoon ground chili powder

⅛ teaspoon cinnamon

Coarse salt

BULGUR PILAF

1 tablespoon olive oil

2 shallots, chopped

1 cup (180 g) bulgur wheat

¼ teaspoon salt

2 cups (475 ml) water

¼ cup (35 g) currants or raisins

⅓ cup (45 g) toasted pine nuts

BOWLS

5 ounces (140 g) firmly packed
baby spinach or arugula

¾ cup (175 ml) Everyday Lemon
Tahini Dressing (see page 66)

Chopped fresh parsley (optional),
for garnish

I love bulgur wheat for its quick cooking time and nutty flavor. Here, I pair it with toasted pine nuts and sweet currants, spice-infused roasted root vegetables, and chickpeas for a bold, colorful, and nutritious tribute to Moroccan flavors. These bowls are especially tasty when smothered with Everyday Lemon Tahini Dressing.

To prepare the vegetables and chickpeas, preheat the oven to 400°F (200°C) and line a baking sheet with parchment paper. In a large bowl, combine the carrots, parsnips, beet, onion, and chickpeas. Drizzle with the oil and toss until evenly coated. Sprinkle with the fennel seeds, cumin seeds, paprika, harissa, and cinnamon and toss again. Transfer the vegetables to the lined baking sheet, spreading them in a single layer (you may need a second baking sheet). Season generously with salt. Bake for about 35 minutes, until the vegetables are very tender and browning at the edges, stirring once halfway through the baking time.

Meanwhile, to make the pilaf, heat the oil in a large saucepan over medium heat. Add the shallots and cook, stirring occasionally, for 3 to 5 minutes, until tender and translucent. Add the bulgur and cook, stirring constantly, for about 1 minute. Stir in the salt and water and bring to a boil over high heat. Lower the heat, cover, and simmer for about 12 minutes, until all of the liquid has been absorbed. Fluff gently with a fork, cover, and let sit for 5 minutes. Stir in the currants and pine nuts.

To serve, divide the spinach among four bowls and top each with one-quarter of the pilaf and the roasted vegetables and chickpeas. Drizzle with the dressing, sprinkle with parsley, and serve right away.

SKILLETS AND STOVETOP

I was originally planning to title this chapter "Skillets," but it evolved to include saucepans, pots, and even baking sheets. What the recipes have in common is that most of the action takes place on the stovetop.

Over the course of the last few years, as I've been juggling graduate school and work, I've come to appreciate recipes that deliver big flavor despite a streamlined cooking process. There's nothing more appealing at the end of a long day than a meal that comes together in a single cooking vessel, and in keeping with that theme, I'm sharing a few of my favorite one-dish recipes, including Creamy Curried Lentils and Quinoa (page 194), Spinach and Gnocchi with White Beans (page 201), and salty, spicy Kimchi Fried Rice (page 198).

These are meals that I can depend on. No matter what's going on, no matter how busy I might be, I can make a big pot of Rice, Beans, Tofu, and Greens (page 181). It's a satisfying dinner, and the investment of time that it demands is minor in comparison to the pleasure and nutrition it delivers.

There are also some meals, like the Golden Beet Risotto (page 175) or the Roasted Zucchini Tacos with Corn and Tofu (page 176), that do demand a couple of cooking vessels or methods but still come to life without too much fuss: you can roast one component while you prepare the other on the stove. Whenever possible, I've streamlined the recipes so that you can reuse the same pots or pans. In my Spanish Quinoa with Tempeh Chorizo (page 185), for example, you'll prepare some easy homemade tempeh "sausage" crumbles, wipe the skillet clean, and proceed with the rest of the recipe.

As always, these recipes aren't only intended to deliver flavor. They're also packed with nutrient-dense ingredients, so that your cooking time will be an investment in self-care.

GOLDEN BEET RISOTTO

This risotto is a lovely example of root-to-stem cooking. Golden beets are roasted until tender and served alongside a simple, creamy spring risotto. The beet greens are chopped and added to the risotto before serving, so no part of the vegetable goes to waste. The dish is both hearty and light, and the Cheesy Hemp Seed Topping gives it a boost of rich flavor. I hate to peel uncooked beets, so I usually choose to wrap them in foil, roast them, and then slip the skins off after they're cooked.

_____

MAKES 4 SERVINGS

1 bunch (3 to 4) golden beets, with greens

5 cups (1.2 L) low-sodium vegetable broth, plus more if needed, at room temperature

1½ tablespoons olive oil

½ white or yellow onion, chopped

1 large shallot, diced

2 cloves garlic, minced

1 cup (185 g) Arborio rice

½ cup (120 ml) white wine

½ teaspoon salt

3 tablespoons (15 g) nutritional yeast

1 tablespoon fresh thyme leaves, or 1 teaspoon dried thyme

1 to 2 tablespoons freshly squeezed lemon juice

Freshly ground black pepper

¼ to ½ cup (60 to 120 ml) Cheesy Hemp Seed Topping (optional; see page 89)

Preheat the oven to 400°F (200°C). Cut the greens off the beets and wash them thoroughly. Let drain well, then cut into thin strips. Wrap each beet in foil. Put them on a baking sheet and bake for about 45 minutes, until fork-tender. Remove the foil and, once the beets are cool enough to handle, rub off the skins under cold running water. Cut the beets into ¾-inch (2-cm) pieces.

Meanwhile, heat the oil in a large saucepan over medium heat. Add the onion and shallot and cook, stirring occasionally, for about 5 minutes, until tender and translucent. Add the garlic and cook, stirring constantly, for 1 to 2 minutes, until the garlic is very fragrant.

Add the rice and cook, stirring constantly, for about 1 minute. Lower the heat to medium-low. Add the wine and cook, stirring frequently, until the rice has absorbed the wine. Add ¾ cup (175 ml) of the broth and cook, stirring constantly, until the rice has absorbed the broth. Continue to cook, adding the broth in ½- to ¾-cup (120- to 175-ml) increments and stirring almost constantly, for 30 to 35 minutes, until the rice is tender; wait until each addition of broth has been almost completely absorbed before adding the next. The risotto should be thick and creamy but still a bit soupy; you may not need to use all of the broth.

When the rice is tender, add the greens and cook, stirring frequently, until completely wilted. Stir in the salt, nutritional yeast, thyme, and lemon juice and season with pepper. Taste and adjust the seasonings if desired. If the risotto has become too thick, add more broth as needed.

Serve right away, topping each serving with the beets and 1 to 2 tablespoons of the hemp seed topping.

ROASTED ZUCCHINI TACOS
WITH CORN AND TOFU

This recipe has a bunch of components, but it comes together easily: the zucchini and corn roast in the oven while you cook the tofu and whip up the bright, tangy chimichurri sauce. Tacos are a warm weather mainstay for me, thanks to their simplicity and flexibility. Much like breakfast tostadas, they're a great vehicle for incorporating whatever plant proteins and vegetables I've got in the fridge.

MAKES 4 SERVINGS OF TACOS, AND 1 CUP (240 ML) OF CHIMICHURRI SAUCE

TOFU

1 (15-oz, or 425-g) block extra-firm tofu, preferably pressed (see page 15)

3 tablespoons tamari

3 tablespoons freshly squeezed lime juice

1 clove garlic, finely minced or grated

1 tablespoon agave nectar or maple syrup

Pinch of red pepper flakes

2 teaspoons neutral vegetable oil, plus more if needed

VEGETABLES

2 zucchini, quartered lengthwise and cut into ½-inch (1.3-cm) pieces

2 cups (310 g) fresh or frozen corn kernels

1 small white or yellow onion, thinly sliced

1 tablespoon neutral vegetable oil

1 tablespoon freshly squeezed lime juice

½ teaspoon ground cumin

Coarse salt and freshly ground black pepper

Preheat the oven to 400°F (200°C) and line a baking sheet with parchment paper.

To prepare the tofu, cut it into 16 rectangular pieces and put it in a nonreactive rectangular baking pan, preferably one large enough to fit the tofu in a single layer. In a small bowl or measuring cup, whisk together the tamari, lime juice, garlic, agave nectar, and red pepper flakes. Pour the mixture over the tofu.

To cook the vegetables, combine the zucchini, corn, onion, oil, lime juice, and cumin in a medium bowl and mix well. Spread the vegetables on the lined baking sheet and sprinkle generously with salt and pepper. Bake for 30 to 35 minutes, until the onion is lightly golden and some of the corn is crispy, stirring once halfway through the baking time.

Meanwhile, to make the chimichurri sauce, combine the hemp seeds, orange juice, lime juice, vinegar, oil, parsley, cilantro, garlic, salt, and pepper in a blender (preferably a high-speed blender) and process until smooth. If the sauce is thicker than you'd like, add water, 1 tablespoon at a time, to achieve the desired consistency. (Stored in an airtight container in the refrigerator, the sauce will keep for 5 days.)

About 5 minutes before the end of the baking time for the vegetables, put the taco shells in the oven to warm them.

To cook the tofu, put the oil in a large skillet or grill pan over medium-high heat. Transfer the tofu to the pan, reserving the

CONTINUED

HEMP CHIMICHURRI SAUCE

¼ cup (40 g) shelled hemp seeds

6 tablespoons (90 ml) freshly squeezed orange juice

1 tablespoon freshly squeezed lime juice

1½ tablespoons red wine vinegar

2 tablespoons olive oil

1 cup (40 g) firmly packed fresh parsley

½ cup (15 g) firmly packed fresh cilantro

1 clove garlic, coarsely chopped

½ teaspoon salt

¼ teaspoon freshly ground black pepper

8 corn taco shells, or 6-inch (15-cm) corn or whole wheat tortillas

½ cup (20 g) chopped fresh cilantro

marinade. Cook the tofu for 3 to 4 minutes on each side, until lightly browned or grilled. Pour the remaining marinade over the tofu and remove the pan from the heat.

To serve, fill each taco shell with about ¼ cup (60 ml) of the vegetables, a few pieces of the tofu, a tablespoonful of cilantro, and a generous drizzle of the sauce.

RICE, BEANS, TOFU, AND GREENS

This dish grew out of my tremendous love of rice and beans, as well as my tendency to load up the dish with extras: greens, peppers, sautéed mushrooms, tofu or tempeh, and whatever else strikes my fancy. I love it because it's fast and filling, and it all comes together in a single pot. I'm the sort of person who can eat plain tofu right out of the package, so adding unmarinated, uncooked tofu doesn't bother me. If naked tofu is a turnoff for you, feel free to use 8 ounces (225 g) smoked or baked tofu instead.

MAKES 4 TO 6 SERVINGS

1 tablespoon olive oil

1 white or yellow onion, chopped

1 small bell pepper, chopped

1 teaspoon ground cumin

1 teaspoon chili powder

½ teaspoon smoked paprika

½ teaspoon salt

1½ cups (270 g) cooked black beans, or 1 (15-oz, or 425-g) can, drained and rinsed

1 (14.5-oz, or 411-g) can diced or crushed tomatoes, preferably fire-roasted

1 cup (185 g) white or brown basmati or long-grain white rice

2¾ cups (650 ml) water

1 (15-oz, or 425-g) block extra-firm tofu, preferably pressed (see page 15), cut into ¾-inch (2-cm) cubes

1 small bunch collard greens or other greens, stemmed and cut into thin strips

Red pepper flakes (optional)

Freshly squeezed lime juice

OPTIONAL TOPPINGS
Crumbled corn chips, chopped fresh cilantro, lime wedges, hot sauce

Heat the oil in a large pot over medium heat. Add the onion and bell pepper and cook, stirring occasionally, for 5 to 7 minutes, until the onion is tender and translucent. Stir in the cumin, chili powder, paprika, and salt, then stir in the beans, tomatoes, rice, and water. Add the tofu and stir gently to combine. Bring to a boil, then lower the heat, cover, and simmer, stirring gently from time to time, until the rice is tender, about 20 minutes for white rice or 40 minutes for brown rice.

Add the greens, cover, and simmer for 5 to 10 minutes, until the greens are wilted. Season with red pepper flakes and stir in lime juice to taste. Taste and adjust the seasonings if desired. Serve right away, with any additional toppings you like.

CREAMY BROWN RICE
WITH SHIITAKES AND PEAS

This creamy rice dish is comforting, like risotto, but it's made with brown rice, rather than Arborio, and the sauce and peas are stirred in after the rice is cooked, which makes the simmering process typical of risotto unnecessary. It's a lovely meal to serve in the spring when fresh peas are in season, but frozen will work at any time of year.

MAKES 4 SERVINGS OF RICE, AND 1 CUP (240 ML) CASHEW CREAM

CASHEW CREAM

¾ cup (95 g) raw cashews, soaked for at least 2 hours and drained

⅔ cup (160 ml) water

¼ teaspoon salt

RICE

1¼ cups (250 g) short-grain brown rice

1 tablespoon olive oil

1 large shallot, chopped

4 cloves garlic, minced

5 ounces (140 g) shiitake mushrooms, stemmed and sliced

Salt

1 cup (140 g) fresh or frozen green peas

½ cup (120 ml) water

2 teaspoons freshly squeezed lemon juice, plus more if desired

Freshly ground black pepper

¼ cup (60 ml) Cheesy Hemp Seed Topping (see page 89)

To make the Cashew Cream, combine all the ingredients in a blender (preferably a high-speed blender) and process until very smooth.

Cook the rice as directed on page 13. While the rice is steaming, heat the oil in a large skillet over medium heat. Add the shallot and cook, stirring occasionally, for about 4 minutes, until translucent. Add the garlic, mushrooms, and a pinch of salt and cook, stirring frequently, for 5 to 7 minutes, until the mushrooms have released their juices and reduced in size.

Meanwhile, bring a medium pot of water to a boil. Add the peas and blanch for about 2 minutes, until bright green and tender. Drain immediately.

Add the peas to the mushroom mixture, along with the rice, Cashew Cream, water, lemon juice, and ¼ teaspoon salt. Season with pepper. Stir well, then taste and adjust the seasonings if desired. Serve right away, topped with a sprinkling of the hemp seed topping.

SPANISH QUINOA
WITH TEMPEH CHORIZO

MAKES 4 TO 6 SERVINGS

TEMPEH CHORIZO

2 teaspoons olive oil

8 ounces (225 g) tempeh, crumbled

2 cloves garlic, minced or finely grated

¾ cup (175 ml) low-sodium vegetable broth

1 tablespoon tamari

¾ teaspoon dried oregano

½ teaspoon smoked paprika

½ teaspoon chili powder

QUINOA

1 tablespoon olive oil

1 small white or yellow onion, thinly sliced

1 red or yellow bell pepper, cut into 2-inch (5-cm) strips

4 cloves garlic, minced

1 (6-oz, or 170-g) jar marinated artichoke hearts, drained and quartered lengthwise

1 (14.5-oz, or 411-g) can diced tomatoes, preferably fire-roasted, drained, or 2 tomatoes, chopped

7 ounces (200 g) green beans, trimmed and cut into 1-inch (2.5-cm) pieces

1 cup (170 g) quinoa, rinsed

2 cups (475 ml) low-sodium vegetable broth

1 teaspoon ground turmeric

2 tablespoons minced fresh rosemary leaves, or 2 teaspoons dried rosemary

¼ teaspoon salt

⅔ cup (90 g) frozen green peas, thawed

Red pepper flakes

Vegan chorizo is easy to find in natural foods stores and supermarkets these days, but it's rewarding to make it from scratch. Combined with quinoa, herbs, artichokes, and tomatoes, the chorizo creates a dish that's reminiscent of paella but can accommodate a weeknight cooking schedule.

To make the chorizo, heat the oil in a large, deep skillet over medium heat. Add the tempeh and cook, stirring constantly, for about 2 minutes, until lightly browned. Add the garlic and cook, stirring constantly, for 1 minute. Stir in the broth, tamari, oregano, paprika, and chili powder. Lower the heat to medium-low and cook, stirring occasionally, for about 5 minutes, until the broth has been absorbed. Transfer the tempeh to a plate, cover, and set aside.

To prepare the quinoa, heat the oil in the same skillet over medium heat. Add the onion and bell pepper and cook, stirring occasionally, for 8 minutes, until the onion is tender and starting to brown. Add the garlic and cook, stirring for 2 minutes. Stir in the artichoke, tomatoes, beans, quinoa, broth, turmeric, rosemary, and salt. Bring to a boil, lower the heat, cover, and simmer for 15 minutes. Add the peas, cover, and cook for 5 minutes.

Remove the lid. If liquid remains, continue to cook until all of it has been absorbed, about 5 minutes. Season with red pepper flakes. Taste and adjust the seasonings if desired. Serve right away, topping the quinoa with the chorizo.

TEMPEH CHORIZO VARIATIONS

Makes about 1¾ cups (8 oz, or 225 g)

Savory Tempeh Sausage Crumbles Replace the oregano, paprika, and chili powder with ½ teaspoon rubbed sage, ½ teaspoon dried thyme, 1 teaspoon dried rosemary, and 1 teaspoon fennel seeds.

Smoky Tempeh Sausage Crumbles Omit the oregano and double the smoked paprika and chili powder.

Tempeh Andouille Crumbles Omit the oregano, double the smoked paprika, and add 1 teaspoon dried thyme and a pinch of cayenne.

BALSAMIC-GLAZED TEMPEH
AND VEGETABLES OVER SOFT POLENTA

Soft polenta topped with a vegetable and some sort of protein is one of my go-to weeknight dishes. In this recipe, the polenta is topped with sweet onions, spicy broccoli rabe, and toothsome seared tempeh, then given a sweet finish with a drizzle of balsamic reduction. The balsamic reduction will seem really tart if you taste it in the pan, but it all comes into balance once it's mixed with the other ingredients.

MAKES 4 SERVINGS

8 ounces (225 g) tempeh, cut into ¾-inch (2-cm) cubes

6 tablespoons (90 ml) balsamic vinegar

1½ tablespoons tamari

1 tablespoon maple syrup

4 cloves garlic, minced or finely grated

Freshly ground black pepper

4 cups (950 ml) low-sodium vegetable broth or water

Salt and freshly ground black pepper

1 cup (140 g) polenta or medium-grind cornmeal

1 tablespoon vegan buttery spread or olive oil

3 tablespoons nutritional yeast

½ cup (120 ml) unsweetened nondairy milk, plus more if needed

1 tablespoon plus 2 teaspoons olive oil

1 white or yellow onion, thinly sliced

1 red bell pepper, cut into thin strips

1 small bunch broccoli rabe, trimmed and chopped

OPTIONAL TOPPINGS
Cheesy Hemp Seed Topping (see page 89) or vegan parmesan, red pepper flakes

Put the tempeh in a shallow glass bowl or container, preferably one large enough to fit all of the tempeh in a single layer. In a small bowl or measuring cup, whisk together the vinegar, tamari, maple syrup, garlic, and a generous grinding of black pepper. Pour the mixture over the tempeh and stir gently to evenly coat.

Combine the broth and ½ teaspoon salt in a large saucepan and bring to a boil over high heat. Lower the heat to medium-low and whisk in the polenta. Cook, stirring frequently, for 10 to 15 minutes, until the polenta is thick and pulling away from the sides of the pan (as it gets thicker, you may need to lower the heat to prevent splattering). Stir in the buttery spread, nutritional yeast, and nondairy milk. Cover the polenta to keep it warm until serving; if it gets too thick, whisk in a splash of nondairy milk.

Heat 1 tablespoon of the oil in a large skillet over medium heat. Add the onion and bell pepper, along with a pinch of salt and pepper, and cook, stirring occasionally, for 8 to 10 minutes, until the onion and pepper are very tender. Add the broccoli rabe and cook, stirring occasionally, for 2 to 3 minutes, until the broccoli rabe is bright green and tender. Transfer the vegetables to a plate.

Heat the remaining 2 teaspoons oil in the same skillet. Add the tempeh, reserving the marinade, and cook, turning occasionally, for about 5 minutes, until gently browned on all sides. Transfer to the plate with the vegetables. Lower the heat to low, pour in the reserved marinade, and cook, stirring occasionally, for 5 to 10 minutes, until thickened and slightly syrupy.

Serve the polenta topped with the vegetables and tempeh, a drizzle of the marinade, and any other toppings you like.

PUDLA
WITH SPICY SAUTÉED SPINACH

Several years ago, vegan blogger and cookbook author Kittee Berns shared a recipe for *pudla*, an Indian pancake made with chickpea flour, that quickly went viral. Thanks to her blog post, *pudla*—especially when it's topped with spicy sautéed greens—has become one of my favorite speedy meals. You can divide the recipe in half or quarter it for a single serving.

To make the pancakes, bring a medium pot of water to a boil. Add the peas and blanch for about 2 minutes, until bright green and tender. Drain immediately.

In a large bowl, whisk together the chickpea flour, baking soda, salt, pepper, turmeric, and cumin. Whisk in the water until the batter is smooth. Stir in the lime juice (the mixture will froth briefly), then fold in the tomato, cilantro, and peas.

Heat 1 teaspoon of the oil in a 10-inch (25-cm) skillet over medium-low heat. Ladle in one-quarter of the batter; it should form a pool about 8 inches (20 cm) across and ¾ inch (2 cm) thick. Cook for about 3 minutes, until bubbles form on the upper surface and the bottom is starting to brown. Use a large spatula to flip the *pudla* (if it gets a little messy, that's fine). Cook for 2 to 3 minutes, until the second side is starting to brown, then transfer to a plate. Repeat three more times with the remaining batter.

To prepare the spinach, trim away the lower stems, then coarsely chop the leaves. Heat the oil in a large skillet over medium heat. Add the onion and cook, stirring occasionally, for 3 to 4 minutes, until the onion is tender. Add the garlic and mustard seeds and cook, stirring constantly, for about 2 minutes, until the mustard seeds begin to pop. Lower the heat to medium-low. Add the spinach in big handfuls, stirring well after each addition. When all of the spinach has been added, cook, stirring occasionally, for 3 to 4 minutes, until the spinach is bright green and tender. Season with salt, red pepper flakes, and lime juice to taste.

Serve the pancakes cut into wedges, topped with the spinach and accompanied by any other desired toppings.

MAKES 4 SERVINGS

PUDLA

1½ cups (210 g) fresh or frozen green peas

2 cups (240 g) chickpea flour

1 teaspoon baking soda

½ teaspoon salt

Pinch of freshly ground black pepper

1 teaspoon ground turmeric

½ teaspoon ground cumin

2 cups (475 ml) water

1½ tablespoons freshly squeezed lime juice

1 small tomato, seeded and finely diced, or 1 small red bell pepper, finely diced

1 cup (30 g) chopped fresh cilantro

4 teaspoons neutral vegetable oil

SPINACH

1 large or 2 small bunches spinach

1 tablespoon olive oil

½ small white or yellow onion, diced

2 cloves garlic, thinly sliced

2 teaspoons mustard seeds

Salt

Red pepper flakes

Freshly squeezed lime juice

OPTIONAL TOPPINGS

Diced or sliced avocado, chutney, hummus, plain unsweetened nondairy yogurt, chopped fresh cilantro or scallions

HERBED CAULIFLOWER STEAKS
WITH LEMON CAPER LENTILS

This is an unfussy, wholesome dinner recipe that still looks and feels fancy. Cauliflower steaks are a great choice for entertaining, as they appeal to vegans, gluten-free folks, and omnivores alike. Capers, shallots, and garlic add sophistication to the accompanying lentils and kale. On its own, this meal is lighter than some others in the book, so feel free to pair it with a cooked whole grain or roasted sweet potato spears for extra staying power.

MAKES 4 SERVINGS

1 large head cauliflower

2½ tablespoons olive oil

4 teaspoons herbes de Provence, or 2 teaspoons each dried thyme and dried oregano

¾ teaspoon coarse salt

¼ teaspoon freshly ground black pepper

1 cup (200 g) dried French green lentils, or 2 (14.5-ounce, or 425-g) cans lentils, drained and rinsed

3 shallots, chopped

3 cloves garlic, finely minced

8 ounces (225 g) white or cremini mushrooms, sliced

1 bunch kale, stemmed and chopped into bite-size pieces

3 tablespoons capers

1 tablespoon finely grated lemon zest

2 tablespoons freshly squeezed lemon juice

OPTIONAL ACCOMPANIMENTS
Cooked whole grain or roasted sweet potatoes, chopped fresh parsley, Everyday Lemon Tahini Dressing (see page 66), Caesar Dressing (see page 94), or your favorite dressing or sauce

Preheat the oven to 400°F (200°C) and line a rimmed baking sheet with parchment paper. Trim the stem of the cauliflower so it can rest on a flat surface. Cut the cauliflower in half crosswise, then cut two 1-inch (2.5-cm) slabs from each half, cutting parallel to the first crosswise cut. (Save the rest of the cauliflower for another use.)

Place the cauliflower on the lined baking sheet. In a small bowl, whisk together 1 tablespoon of the oil, the herbes de Provence, salt, and pepper. Brush the mixture evenly over both sides of the cauliflower steaks. Bake for 30 to 40 minutes, until the cauliflower is golden brown and fork-tender, flipping once halfway through the baking time.

Meanwhile, cook the lentils as directed on page 15. Drain well. (If you're using canned lentils, you can skip this step.)

Heat the remaining 1½ tablespoons oil in a large skillet over medium-low heat. Add the shallots and cook, stirring occasionally, for 1 to 2 minutes, until translucent. Add the garlic and mushrooms and cook, stirring frequently, for 5 minutes, until the garlic is fragrant and the mushrooms have released their juices. Stir in the kale and cook, stirring frequently, for 2 to 3 minutes, until the kale is bright green and tender. Finally, stir in the lentils, capers, lemon zest, and lemon juice. Taste and adjust the seasonings if desired.

Place a cauliflower steak and a generous heap of lentils and greens on each plate and serve with any desired accompaniments.

PASTA AND BROCCOLI RABE
WITH CREAMY ROASTED RED PEPPER SAUCE

I roast countless red bell peppers during the summer months, when they're abundant and sweet. I love adding them to sandwiches, wraps, and salads—and to this wonderful pasta dish. If you don't want to roast the peppers, feel free to use store-bought roasted peppers instead. Either way, they add sweetness to the rich and creamy sauce, which contrasts nicely with the peppery, garlicky flavor of the sautéed broccoli rabe. You can use any pasta you like in this dish, but I think spaghetti and linguine are particularly nice.

MAKES 4 SERVINGS

ROASTED RED PEPPER SAUCE

½ cup (65 g) raw cashews, soaked for at least 2 hours and drained

⅓ cup (80 ml) water

¼ cup (20 g) nutritional yeast

2 tablespoons freshly squeezed lemon juice

1 clove garlic, coarsely chopped

¼ to ½ teaspoon salt

⅛ teaspoon freshly ground black pepper

1 cup (185 g) coarsely chopped roasted red bell peppers

PASTA AND BROCCOLI RABE

8 ounces (225 g) pasta

1 tablespoon olive oil

2 cloves garlic, thinly sliced

12 ounces (340 g) broccoli rabe, trimmed and cut into 2-inch (5-cm) pieces

¼ teaspoon salt

2 teaspoons freshly squeezed lemon juice

To make the sauce, combine all the ingredients in a blender (preferably a high-speed blender), using only ¼ teaspoon salt if using store-bought roasted peppers. Process until smooth.

To cook the pasta, bring a large pot of salted water to boil over high heat. Stir in the pasta, then adjust the heat to maintain a low boil. Cook, stirring occasionally, until the pasta is tender but still firm. Drain well.

Meanwhile, to prepare the broccoli rabe, heat the oil in a large skillet over medium heat. When the oil is shimmering, add the garlic and let sizzle for about 1 minute, until just beginning to brown, stirring gently to prevent burning. Add the broccoli rabe and sprinkle with the salt. Cover and cook for 1 to 2 minutes, until the broccoli rabe has wilted a bit. Remove the lid and cook, stirring frequently, for 7 to 10 minutes, until the broccoli rabe is tender. Stir in the lemon juice.

Add the pasta and sauce and stir gently, until evenly combined. Alternatively, you can toss the drained hot pasta with the sauce and accompany with the broccoli rabe. Serve right away.

CREAMY CURRIED LENTILS
AND QUINOA

It's hard not to love this one-pot dish, a quick-cooking curry that's fragrant, creamy, and nutritious. Curries are a mainstay for me, and this one gets bonus points both for its simplicity and the powerful double dose of plant protein from quinoa and lentils.

MAKES 4 SERVINGS

1 tablespoon coconut oil

1 small white or yellow onion, chopped

4 cloves garlic, minced

1 teaspoon salt

1 tablespoon curry powder

2 teaspoons ground turmeric

1 teaspoon ground cumin

½ teaspoon red pepper flakes

1 cup (200 g) dried green or brown lentils

¾ cup (130 g) quinoa, rinsed

4 cups (950 ml) low-sodium vegetable broth

4 to 5 cups (120 to 150 g) firmly packed, chopped spinach, chard, collard greens, or kale

1 cup (240 ml) full-fat coconut milk or Cashew Cream (see page 182)

2 tablespoons freshly squeezed lime juice

Freshly ground black pepper

OPTIONAL TOPPINGS
Toasted cashews (curry flavored would be a good option), chopped fresh cilantro, lime wedges

Heat the oil in a large pot over medium heat. Add the onion and cook, stirring occasionally, for about 5 minutes, until tender and translucent. Add the garlic and cook, stirring constantly, for 2 minutes.

Stir in the salt, curry powder, turmeric, cumin, red pepper flakes, lentils, and quinoa, then stir in the broth. Bring to a boil over high heat, then lower the heat, cover, and simmer for 25 minutes. If the curry is very thick, you can add ½ cup (120 ml) water to thin it slightly. Add the greens, cover, and cook for 5 minutes, letting the greens steam on top of the curry.

Stir in the greens, then stir in the coconut milk and lime juice. Season with black pepper, then taste and adjust the seasonings if desired. Serve right away, with any additional toppings you like.

STUFFED COLLARD LEAVES
WITH POMEGRANATE DIPPING SAUCE

MAKES 4 SERVINGS

FILLING AND COLLARD LEAVES

1 cup (200 g) freekeh, rinsed

⅔ cup (135 g) dried brown or green lentils, or 1 (15-oz, or 425-g) can lentils, drained and rinsed

1 tablespoon olive oil

1 small red onion, diced

4 cloves garlic, minced

1 tablespoon za'atar spice, or 1 teaspoon each dried thyme and dried oregano

1 teaspoon ground cumin

1 teaspoon ground coriander

½ teaspoon salt

¼ teaspoon smoked paprika

¼ teaspoon freshly ground black pepper

1 to 2 tablespoons freshly squeezed lemon juice

¼ cup (35 g) toasted pine nuts or pumpkin seeds

¼ cup (10 g) finely chopped fresh parsley

10 medium collard leaves, tough ribs shaved down with a paring knife

DIPPING SAUCE

¼ cup (60 ml) water

3 tablespoons tahini

2 tablespoons pomegranate molasses

1 tablespoon red wine vinegar

1 teaspoon Dijon mustard

2 teaspoons agave nectar or maple syrup

1 clove garlic, pressed or finely minced

½ teaspoon salt

Freshly ground black pepper

It took me a while to warm up to collard greens. The recipe that turned me around was surprisingly simple: using raw or gently steamed collard leaves as an easy, nutritious wrap. In this version, collard leaves are stuffed with freekeh, lentils, currants, and toasted pine nuts. The filling is spiked with *za'atar*, a vibrant Mediterranean spice blend of oregano, cumin, sumac, and sesame. I like to serve them with a creamy pomegranate dressing, but you could also use Everyday Lemon Tahini Dressing (see page 66). Note that the recipe calls for ten collard leaves; you'll only use eight of them, but it's a good idea to prepare a couple of extra ones in case any split or fall apart during cooking or rolling.

To make the filling, cook the freekeh as directed on page 13. Cook the lentils as directed on page 15, then drain well.

Heat the oil in a large skillet over medium heat. Add the onion and cook, stirring occasionally, for 5 to 7 minutes, until tender and translucent. Add the garlic and cook, stirring constantly, for 2 minutes. Stir in the freekeh and lentils, then stir in the *za'atar*, cumin, coriander, salt, pepper, lemon juice to taste, and pine nuts. Lower the heat to medium-low and cook, stirring gently, until heated through. Remove from the heat and stir in the parsley.

To cook and fill the collard leaves, bring a large pot of salted water to a boil, then lower the heat to maintain a gentle simmer. Add the collard leaves and cook for about 2 minutes, until bright green and tender. Drain the leaves and pat dry with paper towels or a clean kitchen towel. Lay a leaf on a work surface and pile about ⅓ cup (80 ml) of the freekeh and lentil mixture along the stem of the leaf. Fold the top and bottom of the leaf over the filling, then fold one side over the filling. Roll the leaf up from the folded side toward the unfolded side to make a neat parcel. Repeat with the remaining collard leaves and filling.

To make the dipping sauce, blend or whisk together all the ingredients until smooth.

Serve the stuffed collard leaves with the dipping sauce alongside.

KIMCHI FRIED RICE

This recipe calls for an entire jar of kimchi, which might make you worry that it's unbelievably salty or spicy or both. It's neither, I promise; it's just super flavorful. Because the kimchi is so bold, you don't have to add much else in the way of seasoning, and if you have leftover rice on hand, which is actually better in this recipe, the dish comes together in minutes. Choose any brand of kimchi you like, or make your own. If you buy it, be sure to choose a brand that's vegan, since some contain fish sauce or brined shrimp. I love the Mama O's brand.

MAKES 4 SERVINGS

3 cups (540 g) leftover cooked brown rice, or 1 cup (200 g) short-grain brown rice

1 (16-oz, 450-g) jar kimchi

1 cup (150 g) frozen, shelled edamame, thawed

2 tablespoons neutral vegetable oil

1 bunch scallions, white and pale green parts, chopped

3 baby bok choy, chopped

1 teaspoon toasted sesame oil

2 teaspoons rice vinegar

Tamari, as needed

OPTIONAL TOPPINGS

Toasted white or black sesame seeds or gomasio; julienned carrot or daikon; chopped scallions; pickled ginger; sriracha sauce, Sriracha Mayonnaise (see page 146), or Spicy Miso Dressing (see page 139)

If you don't have leftover cooked rice on hand, cook the rice as directed on page 13 and allow it to cool to room temperature. Drain the kimchi in a colander or sieve, reserving the liquid. Chop the kimchi.

Bring a medium pot of water to boil. Add the edamame and blanch for about 2 minutes, until bright green and tender. Drain immediately.

Heat the vegetable oil in a large skillet over medium-high heat. Add the scallions and cook, stirring frequently, for 2 to 3 minutes, or until tender. Add the bok choy and cook, stirring occasionally, for 2 to 3 minutes, until the bok choy is bright green and tender. Stir in the kimchi and cook for about 1 minute, until heated through.

Stir in the rice, edamame, kimchi brine, toasted sesame oil, and rice vinegar. Cook, stirring frequently, for about 3 minutes, until heated through. Taste and adjust the seasonings if desired; you may want to add vinegar or tamari depending on the acidity and saltiness of the kimchi. Serve right away, with any desired toppings.

SPINACH AND GNOCCHI
WITH WHITE BEANS

This is the ultimate easy pasta dinner, a sauté of vegetables and legumes folded together with freshly cooked gnocchi. It's proof that a simple combination of flavors—in this case sun-dried tomatoes, balsamic vinegar, and garlic—can result in a dish with incredibly lively flavor. I call for gnocchi because it's so hearty and cooks quickly, but you can substitute 8 ounces (225 g) of any type of pasta. I've made this dish with penne, fusilli, and bow ties, and all versions were great!

MAKES 4 SERVINGS

1 tablespoon olive oil, plus more as needed

2 large shallots, thinly sliced

4 cloves garlic, minced

12 sun-dried tomato halves (oil-packed or dry-packed), coarsely chopped

5 ounces (140 g) baby spinach

1½ cups (270 g) cooked cannellini or Great Northern beans, or 1 (15-oz, or 425-g) can, drained and rinsed

1 pound (450 g) vegan gnocchi

1 to 2 tablespoons balsamic vinegar

Salt and freshly ground black pepper

OPTIONAL TOPPINGS
Cheesy Hemp Seed Topping (see page 89) or vegan parmesan, chopped fresh basil, red pepper flakes

Bring a large pot of salted water to a boil over high heat. Meanwhile, heat the oil in a large skillet over medium heat. Add the shallots and cook, stirring constantly, for about 3 minutes, until tender. Add the garlic and sun-dried tomatoes and cook, stirring constantly, for 2 minutes. Stir in the spinach; you may need to do this in batches. Cook, stirring occasionally, for 2 to 3 minutes, until the spinach is wilted. Add the beans and cook, stirring occasionally, for 1 to 2 minutes, until heated through.

When the water is boiling, stir in the gnocchi. Adjust the heat to maintain a low boil and cook, stirring occasionally, for about 3 minutes, until the gnocchi are floating on the surface of the water and are tender. Drain, reserving ½ cup (120 ml) of the cooking water, then stir the gnocchi into the spinach mixture, along with 1 tablespoon of the balsamic vinegar. If the mixture is dry, add some of the reserved gnocchi cooking water. Season with salt and pepper, then taste and adjust the seasonings if desired. You may wish to add as much as 1 tablespoon more balsamic vinegar.

Serve right away, with any desired toppings.

SKILLET CHILI MAC

This recipe combines two of my favorite comfort food dishes—chili and mac and cheese—into one easy, hearty, and crowd-pleasing skillet dinner. To ease preparation on busy evenings, you can make the Cashew Queso Sauce ahead of time.

MAKES 4 TO 6 SERVINGS

1 tablespoon olive oil

1 white or yellow onion, diced

1 green or red bell pepper, diced

1 poblano chile, finely diced

2 cloves garlic, minced

1 teaspoon ground cumin

1 teaspoon chili powder

1 teaspoon dried thyme

Pinch of red pepper flakes

¼ teaspoon salt

1 (14.5-oz, or 411-g) can diced tomatoes, preferably fire-roasted

1½ cups (270 g) cooked black beans, or 1 (15-oz, or 425-g) can, drained and rinsed

1½ cups (270 g) cooked kidney beans, or 1 (15-oz, or 425-g) can, drained and rinsed

8 ounces (225 g) elbow or shell-shaped pasta

1 cup (240 ml) Cashew Queso Sauce (see page 225)

OPTIONAL TOPPINGS
Cheesy Hemp Seed Topping (see page 89) or nutritional yeast, hot sauce, chopped scallions

Bring a large pot of salted water to a boil over high heat. Meanwhile, heat the oil in a very large skillet over medium heat. Add the onion, bell pepper, and poblano and cook, stirring occasionally, for 5 to 7 minutes, until the onion is tender and translucent. Add the garlic and cook, stirring constantly, for 1 minute. Stir in the cumin, chili powder, thyme, red pepper flakes, salt, tomatoes, and beans. Lower the heat, cover, and simmer for 5 minutes.

When the water is boiling, stir in the pasta and adjust the heat to maintain a low boil. Cook, stirring occasionally, until the pasta is tender but still firm. Drain well, then add the pasta to the skillet. Pour in the queso sauce and stir gently until well combined. Taste and adjust the seasonings if desired. Serve right away with any desired toppings.

BARLEY RISOTTO
WITH BUTTERNUT SQUASH AND SAGE

Using pearl barley, rather than hulled, makes this dish quick and easy to prepare on a weeknight. Unlike a traditional risotto, it only needs to be stirred a couple of times, and it requires less than half an hour of simmering from start to finish. The tempeh sausage infuses the risotto with the flavors of fennel and sage, while the butternut squash is a sweet surprise.

MAKES 4 SERVINGS

1 tablespoon olive oil

1 small white or yellow onion, chopped

4 cloves garlic, minced

1 cup (200 g) pearl barley

½ cup (120 ml) white wine or vegetable broth

1 pound (450 g) butternut squash, peeled, seeded, and cut into ¾-inch (2-cm) cubes

¾ teaspoon salt

1 teaspoon ground or rubbed sage

4 cups (950 ml) low-sodium vegetable broth, plus more if needed

2 tablespoons nutritional yeast

1 tablespoon freshly squeezed lemon juice

4 to 5 cups (120 to 150 g) firmly packed, chopped kale, chard, or spinach leaves

8 ounces (225 g) Savory Tempeh Sausage Crumbles (page 000) or store-bought vegan sausage, cooked if necessary

Freshly ground black pepper

Cheesy Hemp Seed Topping (see page 89) or vegan parmesan (optional)

Heat the oil in a large pot over medium heat. Add the onion and cook, stirring occasionally, for 5 minutes, until the onion is tender and translucent. Add the garlic and cook, stirring constantly, for 1 minute. Add the barley and wine and cook, stirring frequently, until all of the wine has been absorbed.

Stir in the squash, salt, sage, and broth and bring to a boil over high heat. Lower the heat, cover, and simmer, stirring every 10 minutes or so to ensure the barley doesn't stick, for about 25 minutes, until the barley has absorbed the liquid and the squash is tender.

Stir in the nutritional yeast and lemon juice, then stir in the greens and cook, stirring occasionally, for 3 to 5 minutes, until the greens have wilted. If the risotto is becoming thicker than you'd like, stir in more broth or water, ½ cup (120 ml) at a time. Stir in the sausage crumbles and season with pepper. Taste and adjust the seasonings as needed.

Serve right away, with a sprinkling of the hemp seed topping.

ALOO GOBI WITH GREEN BEANS

Aloo gobi is a fragrant and filling Indian dish that features cauliflower and potatoes. I like to add dal to my version for extra protein, and I typically serve it over a cooked grain for even more staying power. I recommend serving the dish with a sweet, tart chutney for flavor contrast, as well as plenty of chopped fresh cilantro.

MAKES 4 SERVINGS

1 tablespoon neutral vegetable oil

2 teaspoons mustard seeds

1 teaspoon cumin seeds

1 white or yellow onion, diced

3 cloves garlic, minced

1 tablespoon curry powder

2 teaspoons ground turmeric

⅛ to ¼ teaspoon ground cloves

¾ teaspoon salt

¼ teaspoon freshly ground black pepper

1 small head cauliflower, cut into bite-size florets

1 pound (450 g) russet or red potatoes, peeled and chopped into bite-size pieces

½ cup (100 g) dried chana dal, toor dal, or red or yellow lentils

3 cups (710 ml) low-sodium vegetable broth, plus more if needed

7 ounces (200 g) green beans, trimmed and cut into 1-inch (2.5-cm) pieces

¼ cup (60 ml) full-fat coconut milk

1 tablespoon freshly squeezed lime juice, plus more if desired

OPTIONAL ACCOMPANIMENTS

Cooked basmati rice or quinoa, chutney (mango is particularly good), chopped fresh cilantro

Heat the oil in a large pot over medium-low heat. Add the mustard seeds and cumin seeds and cook, stirring frequently, for 1 to 2 minutes, until the seeds are fragrant and popping. Add the onion and cook, stirring frequently, for 5 to 7 minutes, until the onion is tender and translucent. Add the garlic and cook, stirring constantly, for 1 to 2 minutes, until the garlic is very fragrant.

Stir in the curry powder, turmeric, cloves, salt, pepper, cauliflower, potatoes, and dal, then stir in the broth. Bring to a boil over medium-high heat, then lower the heat, cover, and simmer, stirring occasionally, for 25 minutes. The final dish should resemble a thick stew; if it becomes too thick as it cooks, add more broth as needed.

Use an immersion blender to partially puree the mixture, or puree a portion of it in a standard blender and return it to the pot. Add the green beans, cover, and cook over medium-low heat for 5 minutes. Stir in the coconut milk and lime juice. Taste and adjust the seasonings if desired; you may want to add more lime juice. Serve right away, atop basmati rice or quinoa, with any other accompaniments alongside.

COCONUT AND SCALLION RICE
WITH GLAZED TOFU AND BOK CHOY

MAKES 4 SERVINGS

RICE

2 teaspoons coconut oil

3 scallions, white parts only, chopped

2 cloves garlic, minced or finely grated

1 tablespoon minced or finely grated fresh ginger

1 cup (185 g) white jasmine rice

1 cup (240 ml) low-sodium vegetable broth

¾ cup (175 ml) full-fat coconut milk

½ teaspoon salt

Finely grated zest and juice of 1 lime

TOFU AND BOK CHOY

4 teaspoons neutral vegetable oil

1 (15-oz, or 425-g) block extra-firm tofu, preferably pressed (see page 15), cut into 1-inch (2.5-cm) cubes

2 tablespoons tamari

2 tablespoons maple syrup

1 tablespoon rice vinegar, plus more as needed

2 cloves garlic, minced or finely grated

Pinch of red pepper flakes

3 large or 4 small baby bok choy, ends trimmed and leaves separated

1 tablespoon water

Salt

OPTIONAL TOPPINGS

Sriracha sauce, toasted coconut flakes, toasted sesame seeds, chopped scallions, lime wedges, chopped fresh cilantro

The coconut rice in this recipe is one of my favorites. I often use it as a base for a simple lunch or dinner, piling steamed veggies on top and drizzling with some sort of sauce. I also like to eat it for breakfast; it's similar to Congee (page 54) but richer. Here, it's paired with sweet and salty glazed tofu and quickly sautéed baby bok choy for a particularly satisfying and wholesome meal. I like to serve this dish with toasted coconut flakes and, to offset the sweetness of the rice, a squeeze of sriracha sauce.

To make the rice, heat the oil in a medium pot over medium heat. Add the scallions and cook, stirring frequently, for 3 minutes. Add the garlic and ginger and cook, stirring constantly, for 1 minute. Add the rice and stir until evenly coated. Stir in the broth, coconut milk, and salt. Bring to a boil over medium-high heat, then lower the heat, cover, and simmer for about 15 minutes, until the rice is tender and creamy. Stir in the lime zest and juice. Taste and adjust the seasonings if desired.

Meanwhile, prepare the tofu and bok choy. Heat 2 teaspoons of the oil in a large skillet over medium-high heat. Add the tofu and cook, stirring gently from time to time, for 7 to 8 minutes, until crispy and golden on all sides. In a small bowl or measuring cup, whisk together the tamari, maple syrup, vinegar, garlic, and red pepper flakes, then pour the mixture into the skillet. Cook, stirring gently, for about 3 minutes, until the liquid has thickened and the tofu is well coated. Transfer the tofu to a plate or small bowl, leaving the liquid in the skillet.

Heat the remaining 2 teaspoons oil in the same skillet. Add the bok choy and water and cook, stirring constantly, until the bok choy is wilted and bright green. Taste and adjust the seasonings if desired.

Serve the rice topped with the tofu and bok choy, along with any desired toppings.

DINNER TOAST
WITH SAVORY MUSHROOMS, CHICKPEAS, AND GREENS

I'm almost embarrassed to say how often I eat some form of toast for dinner. But then again, why not? Toast is quintessential comfort food, and there's no reason for it to be bland. This savory toast was inspired by Rebecca Fallihee's killer recipe for mushrooms and garbanzos on toast at the Food52 website. My version includes greens and rosemary, along with a few other adaptations. Packed with umami and quick to prepare, it's a perfect meal for weeknight cooking. Be sure to use sturdy bread so you can soak up all of the soupy, savory goodness of the toppings.

MAKES 4 SERVINGS

1 tablespoon olive oil

2 large shallots, thinly sliced

10 ounces (285 g) shiitake mushrooms, stemmed and thinly sliced

Salt

1½ cups (250 g) cooked chickpeas, or 1 (15-oz, or 425-g) can, drained and rinsed

1 teaspoon smoked paprika

1½ tablespoons finely chopped fresh rosemary leaves, or 1 teaspoon dried rosemary

1 tablespoon fresh thyme leaves, or 1 teaspoon dried thyme

1 tablespoon apple cider vinegar

1½ cups (355 ml) low-sodium vegetable broth

2 tablespoons all-purpose flour

3 cups (90 g) firmly packed, finely chopped kale, spinach, or chard

Freshly ground black pepper

8 slices whole grain bread

OPTIONAL TOPPINGS
Chopped fresh parsley, thyme leaves, balsamic vinegar

Heat the oil in a large skillet over medium heat. Add the shallots and cook, stirring frequently, for about 2 minutes, just until translucent. Add the mushrooms and a generous pinch of salt and cook, stirring occasionally for about 5 minutes, until the mushrooms have released their juices. Stir in the chickpeas, paprika, rosemary, thyme, and vinegar.

In a small bowl or measuring cup, whisk together the broth and flour. Pour the mixture into the skillet and bring to a boil over medium-high heat. Lower the heat and simmer, stirring occasionally, for 5 minutes, until the liquid has thickened into a gravy. Stir in the greens and cook, stirring frequently, for about 3 minutes, until the greens are wilted. Season with pepper, then taste and adjust the seasonings if desired. Remove from the heat.

Toast the bread. Ladle the chickpeas and mushrooms over the toast and serve right away, with a garnish of fresh herbs and a drizzle of good balsamic vinegar.

SPICY CHICKPEA QUESADILLAS
WITH CARAMELIZED ONIONS

This recipe begins with a little hard work: caramelizing onions, which demands time and patience in order to achieve sweetness and depth of flavor. After that, the quesadillas come together quickly. The protein here is a spicy, smoky chickpea mash, similar to hummus but with more texture and a little less richness. To ease preparation, you can use store-bought hummus or caramelize the onions in advance—the caramelized onions can even be frozen until you're ready to use them.

MAKES 4 SERVINGS

1 tablespoon neutral vegetable oil

2 large or 3 small yellow onions, thinly sliced

1 teaspoon brown sugar

¾ teaspoon salt

1 tablespoon balsamic vinegar

1½ cups (250 g) cooked chickpeas, or 1 (15-oz, or 425-g) can, drained and rinsed

2 tablespoons vegan mayonnaise or tahini

1 small clove garlic, minced or finely grated

1½ tablespoons chopped chipotles in adobo with their sauce

½ teaspoon ground cumin

1 tablespoon freshly squeezed lime juice

Salt and freshly ground black pepper

4 large (10-in, or 25-cm) flour tortillas, preferably whole wheat

2 cups (120 g) firmly packed baby spinach

Vegetable oil

OPTIONAL TOPPINGS
Avocado slices, chopped fresh parsley or cilantro, hot sauce, Cashew Queso Sauce (see page 225)

Heat the vegetable oil in a large skillet over medium heat. Add the onions, sugar, and ½ teaspoon of the salt and cook, stirring frequently, for 5 minutes. Lower the heat to medium-low and cook, stirring every 5 to 7 minutes, for 30 minutes, until the onions are deep brown and very soft. Add splashes of water as needed if the onions start to stick. Stir in the vinegar.

Combine 1 cup (150 g) chickpeas with the mayonnaise, garlic, chipotles en adobo, cumin, and remaining ¼ teaspoon salt in a food processor. Process for 30 seconds, or until the mixture is roughly combined. Add the remaining chickpeas and the lime juice. Pulse about 10 times, or until the chickpeas are broken down but still visible. Season with salt and pepper.

Lightly coat a large skillet with oil, and place it over medium high heat. On a work surface, spread half of the chickpea mixture across one tortilla, followed by half of the onions and baby spinach, then top with another tortilla. Transfer the quesadilla to the hot skillet. Cook for 2 to 3 minutes, or until the bottom tortilla is golden and crisp at the edges. Flip and crisp the quesadilla on the second side, then remove it from the heat. Repeat with the remaining two tortillas and filling. Cut the quesadillas into quarters and serve right away.

BAKES

There's a particular type of dish that I think of as a Sunday meal, even though it doesn't need to be served on a Sunday. These recipes demand a little more patience and assembly time than run-of-the-mill dinners, but the payoff is a layered, comforting, and exceptionally hearty meal. I treat these dishes as special projects, putting them together as I take care of other stuff around the house. They're definitely not for busy weeknights!

Many of the recipes in this chapter of baked dishes are quintessential Sunday meals. These are recipes I turn to in the dead of winter, when comfort food is at its most essential. There are few things I'd rather eat on a cold night than Creamy Penne Primavera Bake (page 229), or Black Bean Enchiladas with Roasted Butternut Squash (page 217). This chapter also includes some of my favorite dishes for holidays and special gatherings: the Vegetable Harvest Pie with Tempeh (page 230) has been on my Christmas menu for years now, and it has won over the hearts of even my most meat-loving friends and family members.

Of course, the oven is useful for dishes other than casseroles and time-intensive cooking projects. In spite of the slightly longer cooking times, baking can be a refreshingly hands-off way to prepare a meal. Baked Potatoes with Lemon Garlic Broccolini and White Beans (page 233) is an ideal weeknight dinner because you can prepare the topping quickly while the potatoes bake, and the Baked Millet Polenta with Spicy Red Lentil Marinara (page 221) offers an especially easy way to cook millet.

In other words, you can break out these recipes for special occasions and feasts, but you can also turn to them when you want something homey and comforting that won't demand a lot of babysitting. With any luck, these recipes will give new meaning to the phrase "comfort food."

BLACK BEAN ENCHILADAS
WITH ROASTED BUTTERNUT SQUASH

MAKES 6 SERVINGS

FILLING

1 pound (450 g) butternut squash, peeled, seeded, and cut into ¾-inch (2-cm) cubes

2 tablespoons olive oil

1 teaspoon chili powder

1 teaspoon ground cumin

½ teaspoon smoked paprika

Coarse salt and freshly ground black pepper

1 small white or yellow onion, diced

2 cloves garlic, minced

1½ cups (270 g) cooked black beans, or 1 (15-oz, or 425-g) can, drained and rinsed

1 small bunch curly or Lacinato kale, stemmed and chopped

2 tablespoons freshly squeezed lime juice

Red pepper flakes

ENCHILADA SAUCE

2 tablespoons olive oil

2 tablespoons all purpose flour, whole wheat flour, or spelt flour

1 (8-oz, or 227-g) can tomato sauce

1 cup (240 ml) low-sodium vegetable broth

2 tablespoons tomato paste

1 teaspoon ground cumin

1 teaspoon chili powder

½ teaspoon onion powder

½ teaspoon garlic powder

¼ teaspoon salt

Pinch of cayenne pepper

12 to 14 (6-in, or 15-cm) corn or wheat tortillas, warmed gently

Enchiladas are one of my favorite Sunday suppers. To make the recipe easier, use a store-bought enchilada sauce in place of my homemade version. Garnish with avocado slices, cilantro, and lime wedges, if you like.

To make the filling, preheat the oven to 400°F (200°C) and line a rimmed baking sheet with parchment paper. In a large bowl, toss the squash with 1 tablespoon of the oil, then sprinkle with the chili powder, cumin, paprika, and a generous pinch of coarse salt and black pepper and toss again. Spread on the lined baking sheet. Bake for 25 to 30 minutes, until fork-tender and crisping at the edges, stirring once halfway through baking.

Lower the oven heat to 350°F (175°C). Heat the remaining 1 tablespoon oil in a large skillet over medium heat. Add the onion and cook, stirring occasionally, for about 5 minutes, until tender and translucent. Add the garlic and cook, stirring constantly, for 2 minutes. Stir in the beans, then add the kale a few handfuls at a time, allowing each addition to wilt before you add the next. Cook, stirring frequently, until the kale has wilted completely. Remove from the heat, stir in the squash and lime juice, and season with red pepper flakes and salt to taste.

To make the sauce, heat the oil in a medium pot over medium heat. Whisk in the flour and cook for about 1 minute, stirring constantly. Whisk in the tomato sauce, broth, tomato paste, cumin, chili powder, onion powder, garlic powder, salt, and cayenne. Bring to a gentle boil, then lower the heat and simmer, stirring frequently, for about 5 minutes, until thickened.

To fill and bake the enchiladas, lightly oil a 9 by 13-inch (23 by 33-cm) baking pan and coat the bottom with a scant 1 cup (scant 240 ml) of the sauce. Lay out a tortilla, put about ⅓ cup (80 ml) of the filling across the middle, and roll the tortilla up. Place it, seam side down, in the baking pan. Repeat with the remaining tortillas and filling. Spread the rest of the sauce over the rolled tortillas. Bake for 25 to 30 minutes, until the sauce is dark and the enchiladas are bubbly. Serve hot.

HOME-STYLE STUFFED SHELLS

In addition to being hearty and crowd-pleasing, this pasta dish is a great candidate for making ahead of time (translation: easy entertaining). The tofu-based filling, which recalls a ricotta stuffing, can be prepared up to a day in advance, as can the marinara. The "tofu ricotta" prepared without the spinach is a good, all-purpose cheese alternative: I've been known to prepare it without the spinach and crumble it into salads, in which case it's reminiscent of feta. If you'd like to streamline the preparation and use store-bought marinara sauce, you'll need 3 cups (710 ml) sauce. You can top these stuffed shells with additional sliced basil.

MAKES 4 SERVINGS

MARINARA SAUCE

1 tablespoon olive oil

3 cloves garlic, minced

1 (28-oz, or 794-g) can diced tomatoes

1 teaspoon dried oregano

2 teaspoons sugar or maple syrup

¼ teaspoon red pepper flakes

Salt and freshly ground black pepper

¼ cup (10 g) thinly sliced fresh basil leaves (optional)

SHELLS AND FILLING

16 to 20 jumbo pasta shells

1 (15-oz, or 425-g) block extra-firm tofu, preferably pressed (see page 15)

1 (10-oz, or 285-g) package frozen spinach, thawed and squeezed firmly against a strainer to remove as much moisture as possible

2 cloves garlic, finely minced

1 teaspoon dried oregano

1 teaspoon dried thyme

¼ cup (20 g) nutritional yeast

¾ teaspoon salt

¼ teaspoon freshly ground black pepper

½ teaspoon red pepper flakes

2 tablespoons freshly squeezed lemon juice

To make the sauce, heat the oil in a medium pot over medium-low heat. Add the garlic and cook, stirring constantly, for 1 minute. Stir in the tomatoes, oregano, sugar, and red pepper flakes. Lower the heat and simmer, stirring occasionally, for 7 to 10 minutes, until the sauce has thickened and the garlic is very fragrant. Season with salt and pepper, then stir in the basil. Taste and adjust the seasonings if desired.

Preheat the oven to 350°F (175°C) and lightly oil a 9 by 9-inch (23 by 23-cm) or 7 by 11-inch (18 by 28-cm) baking pan.

To cook the shells, bring a large pot of salted water to a boil. Add the shells and cook, stirring gently occasionally, until tender but still quite firm. Drain well.

To make the filling, crumble the tofu into a large bowl. Add the spinach, garlic, oregano, thyme, nutritional yeast, salt, black pepper, red pepper flakes, and lemon juice. Use your hands to mix everything thoroughly, making sure to evenly distribute the herbs and spices. Taste and adjust the seasonings if desired.

Coat the bottom of the baking pan with 1 cup (240 ml) of the sauce. Stuff each pasta shell with enough of the tofu mixture to fill it up—about ¼ cup (60 ml) filling per shell. Arrange the shells in the baking pan and pour the remaining sauce over the top. Bake for 25 minutes, until bubbly. Serve hot.

BAKED MILLET POLENTA
WITH SPICY RED LENTIL MARINARA

Millet can be a tough sell: a lot of people, myself included, find it to be a little dry when it's prepared traditionally. Cooking millet with extra water or broth—using a one-to-four ratio of grain to liquid—creates a crowd-pleasing mixture that's reminiscent of traditional polenta. In this dish, the millet polenta is baked and topped with a hearty marinara sauce that gets a protein boost from red lentils.

To make the marinara, heat the oil in a medium pot over medium heat. Add the onion and cook, stirring occasionally, for 5 minutes. Add the sugar and cook, stirring from time to time, for about another 5 minutes, until the onion is tender and golden. Add the garlic and cook, stirring constantly, for 2 minutes.

Stir in the oregano, thyme, tomatoes, tomato sauce, salt, pepper, lentils, and water. Bring to a boil, then lower the heat and simmer, stirring occasionally, for 15 minutes, until the lentils are tender. Add the spinach, cover, and let the spinach wilt for 2 minutes. Stir in the spinach, then stir in the red pepper flakes. Taste and adjust the seasonings if desired.

To make the polenta, preheat the oven to 350°F (175°C). Put a 10-inch (25-cm) cast-iron or ovenproof skillet on the stovetop over medium heat. Pour in the millet and toast, stirring frequently, for 8 to 10 minutes, until it begins to brown and pop. Pour the broth into the pan.

Bake the millet for 20 minutes. Stir, then bake for another 20 to 30 minutes, until the millet is firm at the edges and all the liquid has been absorbed.

Remove the millet from the oven and stir in the nondairy milk, salt, pepper, garlic powder, and nutritional yeast. Gently reheat the marinara sauce. Spoon the millet onto four plates and top with the sauce, along with chopped fresh parsley or basil. Serve right away.

MAKES 4 SERVINGS

LENTIL MARINARA

1 tablespoon olive oil

1 white or yellow onion, chopped

1 teaspoon sugar

3 cloves garlic, minced

½ teaspoon dried oregano

½ teaspoon dried thyme

1 (14.5-oz, or 411-g) can diced tomatoes

1 (8-oz, or 227-g) can tomato sauce

¾ teaspoon salt

¼ teaspoon freshly ground black pepper

½ cup (100 g) dried red lentils

1 cup (240 ml) water

2 cups (60 g) firmly packed baby spinach

½ teaspoon red pepper flakes

MILLET POLENTA

1 cup (220 g) millet, rinsed

4 cups (950 ml) low-sodium vegetable broth

1 cup (240 ml) unsweetened nondairy milk

½ teaspoon salt

¼ teaspoon freshly ground black pepper

½ teaspoon garlic powder

3 tablespoons nutritional yeast

OPTIONAL TOPPINGS

Chopped fresh parsley, chopped fresh basil leaves

STUFFED PEPPERS
WITH FARRO, HERBS, AND TEMPEH SAUSAGE

These stuffed peppers are one of my favorite dishes to serve at holidays and family gatherings. The traditional Italian flavors are approachable for everyone, and the dish is filling enough to satisfy robust appetites. To ease the final preparation, you can cook the farro and make the sausage crumbles in advance. To make it even easier, you can substitute store-bought vegan sausage for the homemade sausage crumbles.

MAKES 4 SERVINGS

¾ cup (150 g) pearl or hulled farro

4 red, yellow, or orange bell peppers

1 tablespoon olive oil

1 small white or yellow onion, chopped

1 stalk celery, chopped

4 cloves garlic, finely minced

1 tomato, chopped

1 tablespoon fresh thyme leaves, or 1 teaspoon dried thyme

1 tablespoon chopped fresh oregano leaves, or 1 teaspoon dried oregano

2 tablespoons nutritional yeast

½ teaspoon salt

¼ teaspoon freshly ground black pepper

3 cups (90 g) firmly packed baby spinach or chopped spinach leaves

8 ounces (225 g) Savory Tempeh Sausage Crumbles (see page 185) or store-bought vegan sausage, cooked if necessary, then crumbled

2 tablespoons freshly squeezed lemon juice

8 teaspoons Cheesy Hemp Seed Topping (see page 89), additional nutritional yeast, vegan parmesan, or breadcrumbs

Preheat the oven to 375°F (190°C) and line a rimmed baking sheet or 9 by 13-inch (23 by 33-cm) baking pan with parchment paper. Cook the farro as directed on page 13.

Meanwhile, cut the bell peppers in half lengthwise and remove the stems and seeds. Place the peppers on the lined baking sheet, cut side up, and bake for 15 to 20 minutes, until tender and browning at the edges but not collapsing. Remove the peppers from the oven and lower the oven heat to 350°F (175°C).

Heat the oil in a large skillet over medium heat. Add the onion and celery and cook, stirring occasionally, for 5 to 7 minutes, until the onion is tender and translucent. Add the garlic and tomato and cook, stirring frequently, for 3 minutes. Stir in the farro, thyme, oregano, nutritional yeast, salt, and pepper, then stir in the spinach. Cook, stirring frequently, until the spinach has wilted. Stir in the sausage crumbles and lemon juice. Taste and adjust the seasonings if desired.

Stuff each pepper half with about ½ cup (120 ml) of the farro mixture. Sprinkle 1 teaspoon of the hemp seed topping over each pepper half. Bake for 15 to 20 minutes, until the peppers are completely tender. Serve right away.

SWEET POTATO NACHO FRIES

MAKES 4 TO 6 SERVINGS,
AND ABOUT 1 CUP (240 ML)
OF QUESO SAUCE

SWEET POTATOES

4 medium sweet potatoes, scrubbed and cut into spears

2 tablespoons neutral vegetable oil

½ teaspoon salt

1 teaspoon smoked paprika

1 teaspoon chili powder

1 teaspoon ground cumin

½ teaspoon garlic powder

¼ teaspoon freshly ground black pepper

⅛ teaspoon cayenne pepper

CASHEW QUESO SAUCE

½ cup (65 g) raw cashews, soaked for at least 2 hours and drained

2 tablespoons tomato paste

1 teaspoon chili powder

¼ teaspoon smoked paprika

3 tablespoons nutritional yeast

½ cup (120 ml) water

¼ teaspoon salt

1 tablespoon freshly squeezed lemon juice

FIXINGS

1 cup (150 g) cherry tomatoes, halved

½ small red onion, finely diced

1 Hass avocado, peeled, pitted, and cubed

¼ cup (10 g) chopped fresh cilantro

2 tablespoons freshly squeezed lime juice

½ teaspoon agave nectar or maple syrup

¼ teaspoon salt

1½ cups (270 g) cooked black beans, or 1 (15-oz, or 425-g) can, drained and rinsed

Sweet potato fries are one of my favorite things to eat, and for a long time I wondered how I could transform them from a side dish into a full meal. The answer is to load them up with lots of fixings, including black beans, avocado, and fresh vegetables, and then smother them with a creamy cashew-based queso sauce. The recipe for the sauce is worth doubling and keeping on hand: it's delicious on baked potatoes, nachos, tostadas, or Mexican rice. You can top the fries with any of your favorite nacho fixings, including hot sauce, salsa, and pickled jalapeño chiles.

To prepare the sweet potatoes, preheat the oven to 400°F (200°C) and line two rimmed baking sheets with parchment paper. Put the sweet potatoes in a large bowl, drizzle with the oil, and toss until evenly coated. In a small bowl, stir together the salt, paprika, chili powder, cumin, garlic powder, pepper, and cayenne, adding a bit more cayenne if you like things spicy. Scatter the spice mixture over the sweet potatoes and toss again. Spread the sweet potatoes on the baking sheets in an even layer. Bake, stirring occasionally, for about 35 minutes, until quite crispy.

Meanwhile, make the queso sauce. Combine all the ingredients in a blender (preferably a high-speed blender) and process until totally smooth. If the sauce is thicker than you'd like, add another tablespoonful of water.

To prepare the fixings, put the tomatoes, onion, avocado, cilantro, lime juice, agave nectar, and salt in a medium bowl and toss to combine.

Put the sweet potatoes in a large serving dish. Top with the tomato mixture, then the black beans. Finally, drizzle the queso sauce evenly over the top. Serve right away, with any other desired toppings.

MOROCCAN SWEET POTATOES

By the time you finish preparing these stuffed sweet potatoes, your home will be fragrant with the aromas of cinnamon, garlic, and ginger. The lentils in this dish are a standout—richly spiced, thick, and hearty. Scooping them over tender baked sweet potatoes is a perfect way to transform them into a complete and satisfying meal; I've also been known to serve them over a cooked whole grain, such as millet or rice. No matter how you serve them, I highly recommend topping them with a generous drizzle of Everyday Lemon Tahini Dressing.

MAKES 4 SERVINGS

4 medium sweet potatoes, scrubbed

1 cup (200 g) dried brown or pardina lentils, rinsed

1 tablespoon olive oil

1 teaspoon cumin seeds

1 small white or yellow onion, diced

3 cloves garlic, finely minced

2 tomatoes, chopped, or 1 (14.5-oz, or 411-g) can diced tomatoes, drained

1 tablespoon finely grated or minced fresh ginger, or 1 teaspoon ground ginger

¼ teaspoon ground cinnamon

½ teaspoon sweet paprika

1 tablespoon harissa paste, or 1 teaspoon ground chili powder

½ teaspoon salt

4 cups (120 g) firmly packed baby spinach

Water, as needed

2 tablespoons pomegranate molasses (optional)

½ cup (125 ml) Everyday Lemon Tahini Dressing (see page 66)

OPTIONAL TOPPINGS

Chopped fresh parsley, chopped fresh cilantro, snipped fresh chives or chopped scallions

Preheat the oven to 400°F (200°C) and line a rimmed baking sheet with parchment paper. Put the sweet potatoes on the lined baking sheet and prick each several times with a fork. Bake for 45 to 60 minutes, until fork-tender.

Meanwhile, cook the lentils as directed on page 15. Drain well.

Heat the oil in a large skillet over medium heat. Add the cumin seeds and cook, stirring constantly, for 1 to 2 minutes, until the seeds start to pop. Add the onion and cook, stirring occasionally, for 5 to 7 minutes, until tender and translucent. Add the garlic and tomatoes and cook, stirring frequently, for 1 to 2 minutes, until the garlic is fragrant. Decrease the heat to low and stir in the lentils, ginger, cinnamon, paprika, harissa, and salt, then stir in the spinach. Cook, stirring frequently, until the spinach has wilted, adding water by the ¼ cup (60 ml) if needed to prevent sticking. Stir in the pomegranate molasses. Taste and adjust seasonings if desired.

Cut each sweet potato in half and use a fork to coarsely mash the flesh, still in the skin. Place two halves on each serving plate and top them with a generous scoop of the lentils. Serve right away, with a drizzle of the tahini dressing and the optional fresh herbs.

CREAMY PENNE PRIMAVERA BAKE

Maybe it's the fact that mac 'n' cheese and baked penne were my mom's specialty comfort dishes when I was growing up, or maybe it's the dense, hearty texture, but I love pasta casseroles, and this is one of my favorites. Like traditional pasta primavera, it's loaded with vegetables and enriched with a creamy sauce, but the addition of tomato transforms the sauce into a delightful cross between Alfredo and marinara.

MAKES 6 SERVINGS, AND ABOUT ¾ CUP CASHEW CREAM

CHEESY CASHEW CREAM

⅔ cup (85 g) raw cashews, soaked for at least 2 hours and drained

½ cup (120 ml) water

2 tablespoons nutritional yeast

½ teaspoon salt

2 teaspoons freshly squeezed lemon juice

PASTA AND VEGETABLES

1 small eggplant, diced

Coarse salt

12 ounces (340 g) penne, rotini, or fusilli pasta

1 tablespoon olive oil

3 shallots, thinly sliced

1 zucchini, diced

1 red bell pepper, diced

4 cloves garlic, minced

1 (14.5-oz, or 411-g) can crushed tomatoes

2 tablespoons tomato paste

1 tablespoon chopped fresh oregano leaves, or 1½ teaspoons dried oregano

1 tablespoon chopped fresh rosemary leaves, or 1 teaspoon dried rosemary

Salt and freshly ground black pepper

⅓ cup (45 g) pine nuts, ⅓ cup (80 ml) Cheesy Hemp Seed Topping (see page 89) or vegan parmesan, or ½ cup (55 g) dry breadcrumbs (optional), for topping

To make the cashew cream, combine the cashews, water, nutritional yeast, salt, and lemon juice in a blender (preferably a high-speed blender) and process until very smooth.

To salt the eggplant, put it in a large colander, sprinkle generously with coarse salt, and toss to coat. Let sit for 25 to 30 minutes, then rinse under cold running water. Dry with paper towels or a clean kitchen towel, pressing to extract as much moisture as possible.

To cook the pasta, bring a large pot of salted water to a boil over high heat. Preheat the oven to 350°F (175°C) and lightly oil a 9 by 13-inch (23 by 33-cm) baking pan. When the pot of water is boiling, stir in the pasta, then adjust the heat to maintain a low boil. Cook, stirring occasionally, until the pasta is tender but still firm. Drain well.

Meanwhile, to cook the vegetables, heat the oil in a large skillet over medium heat. Add the shallots, zucchini, bell pepper, and eggplant and cook, stirring frequently, for about 10 minutes, until the eggplant is tender. Add the garlic and cook, stirring constantly, for 2 minutes. Stir in the crushed tomatoes, tomato paste, oregano, and rosemary, then season with salt and pepper to taste.

To assemble and bake the dish, combine the pasta, vegetables, and cashew cream in a large bowl or the pot used to cook the pasta. Stir gently until evenly combined. Taste and adjust the seasonings if desired. Transfer to the oiled pan and scatter the pine nuts evenly over the top. Bake for about 30 minutes, until the top is starting to get crispy. Serve piping hot.

VEGETABLE HARVEST PIE
WITH TEMPEH

This is quintessential holiday fare: hearty, traditional, and a real crowd-pleaser. It's similar to shepherd's pie, but the filling is made with tempeh, kidney beans, and winter vegetables. If you make the filling in a Dutch oven, you can simply spread the potatoes over the cooked filling and bake the pie in the same pot.

MAKES 6 SERVINGS

POTATO TOPPING

4 large Yukon gold potatoes, peeled and quartered

½ cup (120 ml) unsweetened nondairy milk, plus more if needed

2 tablespoons vegan buttery spread or olive oil

½ teaspoon salt

Freshly ground black pepper

FILLING

8 ounces (225 g) tempeh, cut into ¾-inch (2-cm) cubes

2 cups (475 ml) low-sodium vegetable broth

1 tablespoon tamari

1 tablespoon olive oil

3 leeks, white parts only, thinly sliced

4 carrots, peeled and thinly sliced

3 stalks celery, diced

4 cloves garlic, finely minced

½ cup (120 ml) red wine or broth

2 tablespoons all-purpose flour

2 tablespoons chopped fresh rosemary leaves, or 2 teaspoons dried rosemary

1 tablespoon fresh thyme leaves, or 1 teaspoon dried thyme

¾ teaspoon salt

¼ teaspoon freshly ground black pepper

1½ cups (270 g) cooked kidney beans, or 1 (15-oz, or 425-g) can, drained and rinsed

To make the topping, bring a large pot of salted water to a boil. Add the potatoes and cook for about 12 minutes, until tender. Drain well, then return the potatoes to the pot. Add the nondairy milk, buttery spread, salt, and a few generous grinds of pepper. Use a potato masher to roughly mash the potatoes; they don't have to be 100 percent smooth or fluffy. If they're too thick, stir in a bit more nondairy milk. Taste and adjust the seasonings if desired. Cover and set aside.

To make the filling, put the tempeh in a small saucepan. Add 1 cup of the broth and the tamari. Bring to a boil over medium-high heat, lower the heat, and simmer for 10 minutes. Drain well.

Preheat the oven to 350°F (175°C). Heat the oil in a Dutch oven or a large pot over medium heat. Add the leeks, carrots, and celery and cook, stirring occasionally, for 7 to 8 minutes, until the leeks are translucent and the carrots are tender. Add the garlic and cook, stirring constantly, for 2 minutes.

Stir in the tempeh and wine and cook, stirring occasionally, until the tempeh has absorbed the wine. In a small bowl, whisk together the remaining 1 cup (240 ml) broth and the flour, then add to the tempeh mixture. Stir in the rosemary, thyme, salt, pepper, and beans. Cook, stirring occasionally, for about 5 minutes, until the liquid has thickened. Taste and adjust the seasonings if desired.

If baking in the Dutch oven, carefully spread the mashed potatoes over the top; alternatively, oil a 9-inch (23-cm) square baking pan, spread the tempeh mixture in the pan, then carefully spread the mashed potatoes over the top. Bake for about 35 minutes, until the filling is thick and bubbling at the edges. Serve hot.

BAKED POTATOES
WITH LEMON GARLIC BROCCOLINI
AND WHITE BEANS

These loaded baked potatoes, which taste like traditional twice-baked potatoes with an Italian twist, are my go-to meal when I'm craving fast and simple comfort food. The topping comes together quickly and easily in a single pan, so cleanup is minimal. For a crispier top, you can broil the potatoes for a few minutes after stuffing them.

_____

MAKES 4 SERVINGS

4 medium russet potatoes, scrubbed

1 bunch broccolini

1 tablespoon olive oil

2 large or 3 small cloves garlic, very thinly sliced

1½ cups (270 g) cooked cannellini or Great Northern beans, or 1 (15-oz, or 425-g) can, drained and rinsed

Salt

½ cup (20 g) chopped fresh parsley, plus more for topping

1 teaspoon finely grated lemon zest

1 tablespoon freshly squeezed lemon juice

Freshly ground black pepper

4 tablespoons (55 g) vegan buttery spread or olive oil

½ cup (120 ml) unsweetened nondairy milk

8 teaspoons Cheesy Hemp Seed Topping (see page 89) or vegan parmesan, plus more for topping

Preheat the oven to 400°F (200°C) and line a rimmed baking sheet with parchment paper. Put the potatoes on the lined baking sheet and prick each several times with a fork. Bake for 45 to 60 minutes, until very tender when pierced with a fork.

About halfway through the baking time, cut the broccolini florets from their stems; keeping them separate, cut both the florets and the stems into bite-size pieces. Heat the oil in a large skillet over medium-high heat. Add the garlic and cook without stirring for about 1 minute, until just barely browned at the edges. Stir in the beans, broccolini stems, and a pinch of salt. Cook, stirring frequently, for about 4 minutes, until the broccolini stems are tender. Add the broccolini florets and cook, stirring occasionally, for 2 minutes. Stir in the parsley and the lemon zest and juice. Season with pepper, then taste and adjust the seasonings if desired.

Split each potato and coarsely mash the flesh with a fork, still in the skin. Add 1½ teaspoons of the buttery spread, 1 tablespoon of the nondairy milk, and 1 teaspoon of the hemp seed topping to each potato half and mash again. Taste and season with salt and pepper if desired. Serve topped with the broccolini and bean mixture and with additional hemp seed topping and parsley.

SPICED LENTIL TAMALE PIE

This dish combines two of my favorite foods: richly spiced lentils and tender cornbread. It's a wonderful vegan rendition of traditional tamale pie. The cornmeal topping alone is special: it's kicked up with nutritional yeast for a mildly cheesy flavor, corn kernels for texture, and chopped scallions for color contrast.

MAKES 8 SERVINGS

LENTIL FILLING

1¼ cups (250 g) dried brown or pardina lentils

1 tablespoon olive oil

1 small white or yellow onion, chopped

2 carrots, peeled and diced

3 cloves garlic, minced

1 (14.5-oz, or 411-g) can crushed tomatoes, preferably fire-roasted

1 (8-oz, or 227-g) can tomato sauce

2 teaspoons chili powder

1 teaspoon smoked paprika

½ teaspoon ground cumin

1 tablespoon molasses, or 2 teaspoons maple syrup

1 tablespoon tamari

Red pepper flakes

CORNMEAL TOPPING

1 cup (140 g) cornmeal

1 cup (120 g) spelt flour, whole wheat flour, or all-purpose flour

1 teaspoon baking soda

1 teaspoon baking powder

½ teaspoon salt

1 teaspoon apple cider vinegar

1 cup (240 ml) unsweetened nondairy milk

⅓ cup (80 ml) neutral vegetable oil

1 cup (155 g) fresh or frozen corn kernels

2 scallions, green parts only, chopped

2 tablespoons nutritional yeast

To make the filling, cook the lentils as directed on page 15. Drain well.

Preheat the oven to 350°F (175°C). Heat the oil in a 12-inch (30-cm) skillet, preferably ovenproof, over medium heat. Add the onion and carrots and cook, stirring occasionally, for 5 to 7 minutes, until the onion is translucent and the carrots are tender. Add the garlic and cook, stirring constantly, for 2 minutes. Stir in the lentils and crushed tomatoes. In a small bowl, whisk together the tomato sauce, chili powder, paprika, cumin, molasses, and tamari, then pour into the skillet and stir until evenly combined. Season with red pepper flakes, then taste and adjust the seasonings if desired.

To prepare the topping, combine the cornmeal, flour, baking soda, baking powder, and salt in a large bowl and stir with a whisk to combine. In a small bowl, whisk together the vinegar and the nondairy milk; let sit for a minute or so, then stir in the oil. Pour into the cornmeal mixture and stir just until evenly combined. Fold in the corn, scallions, and nutritional yeast.

If you cooked the filling in an ovenproof skillet, carefully spread the cornmeal mixture evenly over the top; alternatively oil a 9 by 13-inch (23 by 33-cm) baking pan, spread the filling evenly in the pan, then carefully spread the cornmeal mixture over the top. Bake for about 35 minutes, until the crust is firm and golden at the edges and the lentils are bubbly. Cut into wedges or squares and serve piping hot.

MEAL PLANS

My approach to food and nutrition is focused on people—their tastes, lifestyles, cultural backgrounds, and health. This makes it hard for me to present meal plans that aren't highly tailored to individual needs. I know from experience, though, that meal plans can be a useful tool.

The goal of these seasonal meal plans is to show you how individual recipes and meals might be mixed and matched in order to create a nutritious, sustainable eating pattern. The plans aren't prescriptive, and they don't include snacks or sides or sweets, so they're not intended to meet all of your nutritional needs. But they do provide a snapshot of how balanced meals can amount to a balanced eating pattern.

Depending on how many people you cook for, you may find yourself with leftovers when you prepare the recipes. With that in mind, I've incorporated some leftovers into the plans for you.

WINTER

	BREAKFAST	LUNCH	DINNER
DAY 1	Shortcut Steel-Cut Oats (with Winter Toppings)	Roasted Cauliflower Salad with Lentils	West African Peanut Stew with Sweet Potatoes and Chickpeas
DAY 2	Shortcut Steel-Cut Oats (with Winter Toppings)	Roasted Cauliflower Salad with Lentils	Quinoa Bowls with Braised Red Cabbage, Tofu, and Brussels Sprouts
DAY 3	Every Day Breakfast Tostadas	Warm Tofu Chop Salad with Peanut Dressing	Stuffed Collard Leaves with Pomegranate Dipping Sauce and Smoky Red Lentil Stew with Chard
DAY 4	Chai-Spiced Millet Porridge with Carrots and Apples	Stuffed Collard Leaves with Pomegranate Dipping Sauce and Smoky Red Lentil Stew with Chard	Kimchi Fried Rice
DAY 5	Chai-Spiced Millet Porridge with Carrots and Apples	Kimchi Fried Rice	Black Bean Enchiladas with Roasted Butternut Squash
DAY 6	French Toast	Black Bean Enchiladas with Roasted Butternut Squash	Winter Salad with Bulgur, Radicchio, and Toasted Almonds
DAY 7	Cauliflower Scramble	Winter Salad with Bulgur, Radicchio, and Toasted Almonds	Macro Bowls with Adzuki Beans and Miso-Glazed Kabocha Squash

SPRING

	BREAKFAST	LUNCH	DINNER
DAY 1	Breakfast Sweet Potatoes with Hummus, Chickpeas, and Greens	Spring Panzanella with Artichokes, Asparagus, Peas, and Lemon Dill Vinaigrette	Creamy Brown Rice with Shiitakes and Peas
DAY 2	Avocado and Tofu Toasts	Spring Panzanella with Artichokes, Asparagus, Peas, and Lemon Dill Vinaigrette	Mediterranean Quinoa Bowls with Roasted Fennel and Black-Eyed Peas
DAY 3	Shortcut Steel-Cut Oats (with Spring Toppings)	Mediterranean Quinoa Bowls with Roasted Fennel and Black-Eyed Peas	Coconut and Scallion Rice with Glazed Tofu and Bok Choy
DAY 4	Shortcut Steel-Cut Oats (with Spring Toppings)	Coconut and Scallion Rice with Glazed Tofu and Bok Choy	Charred Broccoli Salad with Freekeh and Spring Herbs
DAY 5	Gentle Morning Kitchari	Charred Broccoli Salad with Freekeh and Spring Herbs	Spinach and Gnocchi with White Beans
DAY 6	Spelt Biscuits with White Bean Gravy	Pudla with Spicy Sautéed Spinach	Sweet Potato Falafel Bowls with Freekeh Pilaf and Roasted Cauliflower
DAY 7	Spelt Biscuits with White Bean Gravy	Sweet Potato Falafel Bowls with Frekeh Pilaf and Roasted Cauliflower	Baked Potatoes with Lemon Garlic Broccolini and White Beans

	BREAKFAST	LUNCH	DINNER
DAY 1	Skillet-Baked Oatmeal with Summer Stone Fruit	Tortilla Soup and Guacamole Quinoa Salad with Black Beans	Pasta and Broccoli Rabe with Creamy Roasted Red Pepper Sauce
DAY 2	Skillet-Baked Oatmeal with Summer Stone Fruit	Brown Rice Tabbouleh Salad	Roasted Zucchini Tacos with Corn and Tofu and Tortilla Soup
DAY 3	Maple Cinnamon Granola	Green Goddess Bowls	Roasted Zucchini Tacos with Corn and Tofu and Tortilla Soup
DAY 4	Maple Cinnamon Granola	Zucchini Pesto Pasta Salad	Sushi Bowls
DAY 5	French Toast	Deli Bowls with Smashed Chickpea Salad	Zucchini Pesto Pasta Salad
DAY 6	Every Day Breakfast Tostadas	Wild Rice Salad with Cherry Tomatoes, Corn, Green Beans, and Tofu	Creamy Penne Primavera Bake
DAY 7	Hearty Pancakes with Buckwheat and Blueberries	Sesame Citrus Soba Salad	Creamy Penne Primavera Bake

FALL

	BREAKFAST	LUNCH	DINNER
DAY 1	Hash with Root Vegetables and Tempeh	Tuscan Kale Salad with White Beans	Barley Risotto with Butternut Squash and Sage
DAY 2	Hash with Root Vegetables and Tempeh	Dinner Toast with Savory Mushrooms, Chickpeas, and Greens	Marrakech Bowls with Harissa-Roasted Vegetables and Bulgur Pilaf
DAY 3	Apple Ginger Muesli	Masala Lentil Salad with Cumin-Roasted Carrots	Marrakech Bowls with Harissa-Roasted Vegetables and Bulgur Pilaf
DAY 4	Apple Ginger Muesli	Butternut Squash Salad with Red Quinoa and Pumpkin Seeds	Spicy Chickpea Quesadillas with Caramelized Onions
DAY 5	Wholemeal Muffins and seasonal fruit	Butternut Squash Salad with Red Quinoa and Pumpkin Seeds	Aloo Gobi with Green Beans
DAY 6	Savory Turmeric Chickpea Oats	Aloo Gobi with Green Beans	Sweet Potato Bowls with Cilantro Rice and Black Beans
DAY 7	Whole Grain Waffles	Sweet Potato Bowls with Cilantro Rice and Black Beans	Pudla with Spicy Sautéed Spinach

ABOUT THE AUTHOR

Gena Hamshaw is the author of the blog *The Full Helping*, which she started in 2009. She is also the author of two cookbooks, *Choosing Raw* and *Food52 Vegan*; is a regular columnist for the website Food52; and she has contributed to or been featured in *Self*, *Shape*, *Slate*, the *Washingtonian*, *Redbook*, *O* magazine, and more. Gena works as a nutrition counselor and is completing her master of science degree in nutrition and education at Teacher's College, Columbia University. She lives in New York City.

© James Ransom

ACKNOWLEDGMENTS

Writing this book has been a labor of love, and it wouldn't have been possible without a lot of support.

First, I owe an enormous debt of gratitude to my team of recipe testers, whose feedback made every recipe in this book so much stronger. Thank you for your time, energy, and generosity in helping me. I couldn't have done it without you. Special thanks to Katie Hay for her dedication, her sensitivity to the book and its meaning, and her assistance with retests.

I'm indebted to the wonderful team at Ten Speed Press, especially my editor, Kelly Snowden, who shepherded the book with wisdom and grace. Kelly, thank you for being so perfectly attuned to what I was trying to accomplish with these recipes, and for your humor and patience. Working with you has been an enormous pleasure.

Huge thanks to Jasmine Star for her detailed, intelligent copyediting, and to Kate Bolen for making the production process so streamlined and efficient. Thank you to Emma Campion and Serena Sigona, who turned the book into something beautiful and evocative, and to Angelina Cheney for her elegant design. Thanks to my publisher, Aaron Wehner, for believing in the book, and to the marketing and publicity team at TSP, especially Allison Renzulli and Erin Welke, for helping it to find readers.

I quite literally could not have written *Power Plates* without my dear friend, photographer Ashley McLaughlin, who brought the food to life and worked tirelessly with me through the final month of her pregnancy. Ashley's artistic vision, work ethic, and steady support made this project possible, and I am so grateful. Thanks also to our talented collaborator, chef Benjamin Burke, who prepared all the recipes and whose feedback helped to make them better.

Thanks to my soul friends, Jordan Heimer and Sam Douglas, whose presence in my life is a blessing. Thanks to Chloe Polemis, Kathy Patalsky, Anne Mauney, Christina Wilson, Sam Aronoff, Brendan Brazier, Blanche Christerson, and Kathleen Malliarakis for their love and support. And a big thanks to my mom for cheering me on and taking pride in what I do.

I'm inspired to keep creating and sharing food by all of the incredible activists, cooks, bloggers, and writers in the vegan community. Thank you for the work you do to speak for animals and spread a compassionate message.

Finally, I want to thank the readers of my blog, who have given me the strength and inspiration to make and write about food for nearly a decade now. I'm continually humbled by your generosity, wisdom, patience, and goodwill. Thank you for helping me to celebrate food and its many gifts, week in and week out. This book and its recipes are for you.

INDEX

Published in the United States by Ten Speed Press,
an imprint of the Crown Publishing Group,
a division of Penguin Random House LLC, New York.
www.crownpublishing.com
www.tenspeed.com

Ten Speed Press and the Ten Speed Press colophon
are registered trademarks of Penguin Random House LLC.

Library of Congress Cataloging-in-Publication Data
Names: Hamshaw, Gena, author.
Title: Power plates : 100 nutritionally complete, one-dish
  vegan meals for balanced living / by Gena Hamshaw.
Description: First edition. | New York : Ten Speed Press, [2018] |
  Includes bibliographical references and index.
Identifiers: LCCN 2017029178 (print) | LCCN 2017037609
Subjects: LCSH: Vegan cooking. | One-dish meals. |
  LCGFT: Cookbooks.
Classification: LCC TX837 (ebook) | LCC TX837 .
  H323 2018 (print) | DDC641.5/636-dc23
LC record available at https://lccn.loc.gov/2017029178

Hardcover ISBN: 978-0-399-57905-9
eBook ISBN: 978-0-399-57906-6

Printed in China

Design by Angelina Cheney
Servingware by Fefo Studio, Speck & Stone,
  Humble Ceramics, Sheldon Ceramics,
  and Henry Street Studio

10 9 8 7 6 5 4 3 2 1

First Edition